To Richard
Jenn
Victoria Warneck

River of Memories

"He will wipe every tear from their eyes. There will be no more death or mourning or crying or pain, for the old order of things has passed away." Revelations 21.4

Victoria Sielicki Warneck
Carole Reno Brier

ISBN: 1517516757
ISBN-13 978-1517516758

DEDICATION

For my three children and my grandchildren: Daniel, Jackie, Diana, Daniela, Lauren, Jon Jr., Austin and Nicole. I love you forever.

You are descendants of brave, freedom-loving people who survived worldwide madness, and had the faith and courage to begin again in a new land.

ACKNOWLEDGEMENT

The authors gratefully acknowledge the original cover art created and painted by Muriel B. Lanciault.
www.blart.com

CONTENTS

In the Beginning

Memories of my family and my homeland of Poland run like a river through my days and nights. Sometimes they are as strong as a fast rivers' current, while others tumble over and around rocks, and what I remember is as choppy as the water. Painful reminders arrive when I least expect them. Sometimes they float into my consciousness from the shadows of a dream, unbidden.

On August 23, 1934 when my sister, Leocadia, was six years old, I was born. My parents named me Victoria, and we lived in the village of Derazno, Poczta Derewno, Poland on their farm. Adolf, my father, my mother Helena, Leocadia, and I were part of the extended Sielicki family. Our Grandmother Evelina dubbed Leocadia "Lodzia" at her birth and the nickname stuck.

I often dream of the stream that ran alongside our land. By November, the creek froze solid enough for fast skating. Lodzia and I skated until our noses ran, our cheeks were red as tomatoes, and our feet and fingers numb. Long before the river's ice melted in the spring, we ditched our shoes and itchy wool stockings and dipped our toes in the freezing water. The iciness of the water stung our legs. When we couldn't endure the cold any longer, we raced back to the warmth of our little house. In summer, the creek gurgled and sputtered while we played on its banks. On warm, lazy afternoons, we lay in the thick green grass with the sun shining on our faces, listening to the babble of running water. I thought summer never ended. I was the family's baby and a skinny, sickly child. Someone was always trying to fatten me up with cookies and candy, or other sweet treats. I was a tow-headed youngster, and my eyes greenish-blue.

For generations Sielicki men farmed the land. My mother's ancestors came from the village of Derazno too, and her roots went deep. I had many cousins, aunts and uncles who lived close by.

My grandmothers lived very near to us. My mother's mother, Maria, lived at one end of the village with her daughter Amelia and Amelia's husband, Joseph. Henry and Maria were their children. After the War, Aunt Maria sent Henry to find us. My Grandmother Evelina, Daddy's mother, lived with his two younger brothers, Edwin and Alexander across the road. I spent a lot of time with my grandmothers. I loved visiting each of them. Sometimes I took a loaf of bread, vegetables from the garden, or a dish of pierogis. Both of my grandmothers were guiding lights in my early life, each widowed many years before my birth. The extended Sielicki family led comfortable, satisfied lives. Grandmother Maria knitted mittens and hats for her grandchildren, but she saved the best treat for me. She took a small piece of ham skin with fat on it and wrapped it in a square of fabric tied up with red woolen yarn. That bit of ham was chewing gum before chewing gum came to Poland.

I loved and respected my father. He was a proud man, and it showed in his manner and behavior. He was sturdy and resilient. His hair was the color of strong coffee, and a lock of hair fell across his forehead. When he laughed, his brown eyes reflected merriment. Oh, how he loved a good joke. Lodzia and I adored him. Mom wore her long dark hair parted in the middle and pulled back into a bun. I remember that her hands were rough and red from hard work. She was a two inches taller than Daddy, but it didn't matter. They loved each other. My father didn't cook, and he didn't do household chores. Soft-spoken and thoughtful, he rarely raised his voice. One time when I was little,

I wanted a stick to play with and Daddy had recently planted three willow trees in our yard. I broke a few small branches off the saplings. When he found the damage I caused, he used them to give me a few little swats across my bottom. Mom scolded and yelled at us, the way mothers do when children exasperate them. She was the real disciplinarian in our family.

****

Most men smoked cigarettes and Daddy was no exception. He was a heavy smoker. He grew his own tobacco supply and cured it by hanging the leaves in the attic. He rolled cigarettes in thin paper, scooping up any dropped tobacco and putting it back into his pouch. Later when he couldn't get the thin cigarette paper anymore, he used pieces of newsprint. As the political news got worse, and the threats to Poland continued to escalate he smoked more. A whiff of cigarette smoke always reminds me of my father. He paid a high price for his habit though; he died of cancer a few years after we arrived in the United States.

Daddy's pride and joy were two splendid horses he called Kara and Kasztanka. When he hitched those horses to the buggy and we rode to church or town, people stopped us to admire the handsome pair. Daddy enjoyed the attention. My father and his horses were famous throughout the parish. He took loving care of his family, his animals and his farm. Two years before the War, Daddy bought a piece of land near the larger town of Derewno. He planned to build a modern house for us, and far into the future give land to Lodzia and me as wedding gifts. He wanted to keep his family close.

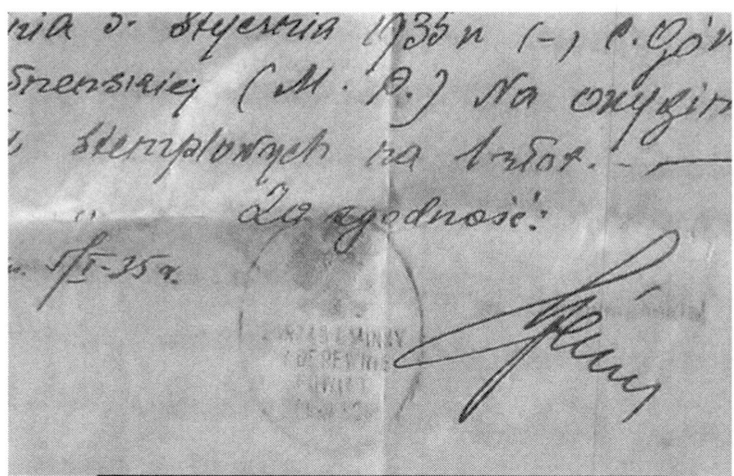
...nia 5. Stycznia 1935 r. (-) ...
... (M. P.) Na oryginale ...
... stemplowych na 1 złot. —
Za zgodność:
... 7/I-35 r.

This is a partial image of the land transfer document. Warneck private collection

My father wearing his Polish Army Uniform. Warneck private collection

****

Our kitchen is the brightest memory of family life in Poland. The yeasty aroma of baking bread reminds me of my Polish family. While Mom kneaded the dough, Lodzia churned the butter. As the dough worked, rising in a warm place, Mom scraped ashes out of the oven and stoked its fire. The oven she used was big; similar to those used in modern pizza shops. Today, if I could have anything in the world, I would ask for a slice of my mother's fresh bread with creamy butter slathered on it. She was a wonderful cook.

One of my favorite meals was green borscht made with *szczaw*. It is a green similar to sorrel, but it has longer leaves and a sour bite. *Szczaw* grew wild in a swampy area near the creek. My job was to pick the greens. Mom cooked a ham bone or kielbasa, potatoes, lots of onions, and some carrots for the broth. Adding *Szczaw* to the pot last. Each bowl received a topping of heavy cream. In summer we had cold borscht made with *Szczaw* topped off with hard-boiled eggs and chopped cucumbers.

She made delicious doughnuts called *pączki* plus a light, sweet pastry filled with nuts and raisins called *babka.* She baked special pastries from old family recipes for celebrations and holidays. People asked "Helena will you make *pączki*?" Or "Helena will you bake *babka*?"

Her breads and doughnuts were famous throughout the village Mom made *nalisniki* for us. *Nalisniki* is a kind of skinny pancake, similar to a crepe, filled with what is on hand. Today, I make them for my grandchildren.

Celebrations or parties filled our house with friends and relatives, and everyone went home with a full stomach.

Mom often hummed or sang a melody while she worked, and soon Lodzia and I joined her. She had a lovely singing voice, and she taught us Polish folk songs and Christmas Carols. Dancing was another of our favorite pastimes. Mom, Lodzia and I danced in the house when the weather was poor, outside when it was nice. My sister went to school and as she learned new songs and dances, she taught me. I learned the alphabet with Lodzia's help. Daddy either couldn't or wouldn't dance, and we teased him by begging him to dance with us. He would throw up his hands and leave for a chore he suddenly remembered. We laughed.

****

We had no electricity or running water, but you don't miss what you've never had. A large wooden barrel near the house's entry held the family's water supply. Water came one bucket at a time. A sturdy door opened into a storage chamber by the kitchen. Constructed from heavy stone, the room kept butter, cheese and milk cold and fresh through the hot summer months. We stored potatoes, carrots, and turnips in a root cellar near our barns. Our animals and the grain we grew kept us well fed. We were never hungry then. My parents were hard-working, modest people who taught us by example. Our lives centered on faith, family, and friends. In Poland, women handled domestic chores and worked side-by side with their husbands. When the wheat was ripe, my father cut it using a swinging scythe. I have always thought of it as a "singing scythe" because of the humming sound it made in use. Mom walked behind him tying up the sheaves. The harvested wheat went into the barn where Daddy separated the wheat from seed coverings. Dry casings of the wheat, called chaff, fed our animals over the winter.

The village miller ground the wheat into flour. Fast running water from two creeks turned the massive stone grinding wheel. The creek flowing behind our house was one of his water sources. Years later the miller's daughter, her name was Leocadia too, found my mother in the United States and came to visit. Given everything that our two families endured, I count this as a miracle.

My parents were never idle unless to sleep. In winter, Mom sat in front of the fireplace spinning flax into fine linen thread and weaving the thread into fabric. Daddy grew the flax. In the fall, he pulled the plants up by the roots and laid them out to let the dew soak them. Wetting the plants made it easier to separate the linen fibers from the plant's woody centers. Daddy combed out the seedpods and saved them for the following years' planting. Mom created tablecloths, sheets and pillowcases from the linen she wove. Mom worked inch by inch and the fabric was delicate and finely crafted. She wove subtle patterns into the cloth. In summer, we took what she had completed outside and soaked it in water from the creek. We spread the wet linen out on the fresh, green grass where the strong summer sun bleached the cloth pure white. Mom sold the linens, butter, and cheeses at the market in Derewno. The viciousness she saw one day at the market stayed with her for the rest of her life.

****

Each year several women, including my mother and Grandmother Maria, went on a retreat to the cathedral in Wilno. The Bishop welcomed them, and they spent three days in prayer.

Another time Mom and Daddy went to Bialystok to buy a part that Daddy needed for his plow. They were gone for about three days. While they were away, I pestered Lodzia.

"When will Mom and Daddy be home?"

At last, I saw the wagon and ran to meet them.

"I missed you, Mom."

"I missed you too," she said.

When you are a child, time moves with the speed of light or drags on for eternity. There is no ordinary time.

****

One large fireplace heated our small house, and the old red bricks surrounding the hearth covered the north wall. Firewood came from a nearby forest. Daddy took his horse and wagon and felled trees, lopped off the limbs and branches, and brought the wood back to the farm. He split the logs and stacked them to dry. It took a lot of fuel to keep us warm all winter.

On a day in early fall, that I shall never forget, my father sharpened his ax and went into the forest. On this day, he was alone. Several hours later, his team pulled the half-empty wagon into the yard. Daddy's face was gray and wet with sweat.

"A viper bit me."

Swelling from the bite had travelled to just below his knee. The nearest doctor was miles away. Word of Daddy's snakebite spread through Derazno at lightning speed. Friends and relatives came to give advice and offers of help. I don't remember one neighbor woman's name, but she was wise in the ways of folk medicine.

She said, "Tie his belt around his leg. Make it tight to stop the poison. If the venom gets to his heart, it will kill him. Make a poultice of sour milk and put it on the bite."

Mom followed her directions. Soon the swelling diminished, and the threat to his heart subsided.

His full recovery from the snakebite took several weeks. The idleness of staying in bed and being quiet made him frustrated and grouchy. My father was unhappy about his family shouldering his responsibilities. My uncles and cousins came every day to care for our farm and animals while he mended. The viper wounded his pride and his leg. My father nearly died from the bite.

****

Deep snow covered the hills by the end of November. Red cheeks and chapped hands confirmed we had been sledding on Derazno's hills. I played in the snow until dusk or frozen toes and fingers insisted on warmth and dry clothes. I had a navy blue winter coat lined with lamb's fleece. I wore it sledding and crashed into a prickly bush. A long, ragged tear opened along one seam. The rip in my coat hurt more than the fresh scrapes and scratches on my face and knees. I went home to Mom who mended it with such neat stitches the rip became invisible. I expected a scolding for carelessness and the holes in my wool stockings.

She shook her head and smiled at me, "Be careful when you go sliding."

****

My parent's faith was very strong. Every week we attended St. Mary's Catholic Church, two kilometers from Derazno. St. Mary's was the home parish for Catholics from neighboring towns and villages. Century's earlier parishioners built the church and its surrounding wall from granite quarried in western Poland. The land the rectory stood on featured an orchard and a sizable garden. In the summer, we had picnics on the grass. Most often, we walked to church, but by October or early November, ice and snowy roads made going on foot impractical and unsafe. When the weather did not cooperate, Daddy hitched his horses to the wagon, and we bundled up for the trip. Parishioners tied their horses and wagons to one of many spruce and oak trees inside the wall. Cars and trucks were uncommon in Poland during the 1930s, horse and buggy, and feet were the primary modes of transportation.

Inside St. Mary's a raised altar presided over two smaller ones. Our priest, Father Karyl, celebrated mass in Latin at the raised altar. Clergy or important visitors sat on three benches near the priest. Regular parishioners stood throughout the service. In summer, the church was cool, in winter it was freezing. Our family stood on the left side of the aisle near the Hail Mary altar. When I was small, I sat on a low set of stairs near my mother's feet.

My parents knew every parishioner. As a coincidence, years' later the boy who became my son-in-law had parents who belonged to St. Mary's Catholic Church. We attended his parent's wedding when I was a small child. The bride's sister was near my age and we played outside that afternoon with the other kids. We played Polish games, hide-and-seek, or tag. Mostly, we ran in and out of the reception space getting underfoot and eating the wedding treats.

****

I was a skinny, boney four-year-old even though I ate everything in sight. Mom watched me eat and yet I stayed scrawny. My arms and legs looked like four small sticks and I developed a pot belly. She talked to the midwife, the closest person in the village to a doctor. The midwife diagnosed intestinal worms. To get rid of them she told Mom to boil a bucket of water and pour sugar and honey into it, mix it up, and have me sit over the bucket before I ate breakfast. We tried her remedy, and it worked. I passed a half a dozen pinworms. Alternative medicine did the trick, and I gained weight. My limbs filled out, and my tummy bulge disappeared.

****

Tommy, the tailor's son, and I played together. Sometimes Sozia, a slight, dark haired, girl our age joined us. My mother heard through the Derazno grapevine that Sozia suffered with seizures, and she worried about us playing together. The current belief was that evil spirits entered the body and caused convulsions. She feared a demon might jump from Sozia to me. One day as we were playing, and without warning, Sozia's body stiffened. She fell to the ground, her body twitching and trembling. Her father appeared out of nowhere, scooped her up and took her away. I ran home crying afraid for Sozia and for myself. Sozia did not play with us after that incident, and I never learned what happened to her after the War started.

****

We were a close-knit family. My father had two younger brothers, Edwin and Alexander. Edwin was the youngest born late in my grandparents' life. He was just twelve years older than me. Alexander, the middle son, married before the War.

My father's uncle, Mihal, lived across the road. He and his wife had three children, Jan, Amilia, and Tomek. Tomek was the youngest. When Mihal's wife died, friends and family sang hymns and kept vigil through the night. I remember going to the wake with my mother. The next day the priest came and they buried Mihal's wife in Derazno's cemetery.

A year after Mihal's wife died he met a young woman from another village named Rosali. Uncle courted her. They married and he brought his bride home to Derazno. Two months after their joyful wedding, Rosali left Mihal and went back to her village. Mihal brought her back. A few months passed and she left Mihal again.

Incensed and embarrassed, Mihal had had enough of her foolishness. Once more, he hitched up his horse and buggy and brought her back.

On the trip back, he told her, "Listen Rosali, if you run away again, I will drag you through the village and tell everyone you deserted your husband and family."

Rosali knew Mihal meant every word he said. So even though she was unhappy in Derazno she stayed with her husband and never left him again. My father teased Mihal about Rosali's rejections for years.

Holidays at Home

Late in the fall, October or November, my parents always slaughtered a pig. The whole family came to our farm and made sausages and kielbasa out of the fresh pork. They took the meat to the village smokehouse for curing.

My uncles, Edwin and Alexander distilled vodka every year in late November for consumption over the holidays. On a cold fall afternoon, I wandered over to visit Grandmother Evelina. My uncles were busy working at their still.

"What are you doing, Uncle Alexander?"

"Making something good to drink at Christmas," he said.

"Can I have a taste?"

"Sure Victoria, here this will warm your belly," and he gave me a sip of vodka off a spoon.

Uncle Edwin watched the exchange laughing.

Homemade vodka burned my throat. I coughed and choked, for several minutes. Then, feeling light and giddy I fell in the snow and laughed. Standing up was a problem so rolled down the hill. Mom watched me through the window, watching me fall, get up, fall down and roll down the hill. She knew my Uncles had given me a taste of the vodka they were distilling. At home, Mom settled me in front of the fire, and I fell asleep. The next time Mom saw her brothers-in-law she scolded them. "Don't you know she's only four years old? What were you thinking? You could have killed Victoria."

****

Dzień Boże Narodzenie means Christmas Day. One Christmas tradition called for serving twelve different dishes. Smoked meats were a special treat. We ate ham, bread, beets and horseradish. We ate scalloped potatoes and doughnuts. Christmas Eve or *Wigilia* was the holiest observance of the year. We celebrated with lovely traditions and paid attention to centuries-old superstitions. For me, the winter holiday interval remains the loveliest time of the year.

Anticipation of Christmas began with Advent and housecleaning. Superstition warned that if the house were dirty on Christmas Eve, it would be dirty for the rest of the year. Mom, Lodzia and I swept or scrubbed every inch except for a little dust left in a dark corner. We didn't want to sweep out the house's luck.

On Christmas Eve day, my father went to the forest, found the perfect tree, and pulled it through the snow to our house. My sister and I decorated the fragrant pine with homemade paper decorations, apples, and pinecones.

When the first star brightened the evening sky, we ate *kolacia wigilia*, Christmas Eve dinner. When we sat down we bowed our heads and Daddy said the blessing. The first Sunday of Advent Catholic priests distributed unleavened bread wafers, called *oplatek*, to parish families. The religious and clergy baked them for a Christmas Eve ritual known as "the breaking of the bread." Daddy handed the wafer to Mom. He wished her good health, and success, and told her he hoped her dreams came true in the New Year. Mom thanked him, broke the wafer in half, and ate a piece. She gave it back to him offering her hopes and wishes for his future. He broke the *oplatek* and ate another piece. Then he gave the wafer to Lodzia, who wished our parents good health and a good harvest, and handed it back to my father, who gave it to me. This age-old tradition began with the eldest and ended with the youngest.

There was no meat served on Christmas Eve. The celebratory dinner might be ruby red beet borscht swimming with dainty dumplings called *uszka*. Many different varieties of finely chopped mushrooms, hard-boiled egg whites, and spices served as fillings for the *uszka*. Then they were cooked in a pot of boiling water. *Uszka* resembles ravioli. It was a happy family meal made memorable by the abundance of love in our home.

Mom placed a tiny bundle of hay at our table to remind us Christ was born in a manger. She set a place at the table for the unseen guest. After supper, my father read the nativity story from St. Luke's Gospel and we sang carols until it was time to leave for church.

Christmas Day we visited friends and family. We called on my grandmothers and stopped to see my uncles and cousins. Mom and her sisters made special savory dishes and fancy cookies and pastries for the holiday gatherings. Daddy and his brothers imbibed in a drink of vodka or rum. I danced and played while the grown-ups talked on a day with no extra work. Most of the talk concerned Hitler and Germany, and what the Third Reich was planning. I wasn't yet old enough to understand. Christmases prior to 1939 are my warmest childhood memories.

****

When Lent arrived in the spring, we cleaned house from top to bottom again. Some warm years pink, yellow and blue wildflowers bloomed in the fields, and Lodzia and I picked bouquets to fill the house with the sweet perfume of spring. Ash Wednesday began forty solemn days of fasting and prayer and ended with a triumphant sunrise Mass ushering in the joy of the Resurrection.

Holy Saturday morning we gathered two dozen eggs. Mom drew crosses and flowers, or she wrote a wish for good health and prosperity on raw eggs using wax drippings from a lit candle. She put them in cold water with sweet onionskins and brought the pot to a boil. The onionskins dyed the shells light brown, and her hand drawn patterns decorated each egg. Decorated hardboiled eggs are *pisanki* in Polish. Mom boiled the second dozen, allowed them to cool, and my sister and I drew designs on them using colored pencils. Holy Saturday afternoon we took a basket with samples of our Easter meal to the church for the *swienconka,* the Easter blessing of the food.

Mom bought colorful cotton fabric and had spring dresses made. I'd dance and swirl around showing mine off. When Easter came early, as it does in some years, and snow still lay on the ground we wore wool stockings underneath our dresses and heavy sweaters on top. Girls and women didn't wear pants or slacks in those days.

The Monday after Easter was a holiday spent with family and friends. Boys and girls played a game using hard-boiled eggs. Two opponents faced each other. One end of the boiled egg stuck out. The players smacked the eggs together, and the player whose eggshell cracked first lost. The loser had to give his egg to the winner. Sometimes I went home with several eggs and sometimes I went home with none. It was fun, too, because my father liked to play. On the second day of the holiday, the boys sprinkled perfume on the girls they liked and tried to steal kisses. In Polish the word for kiss is *Dingus*, thus everyone called it *Dingus Poniedziałek*, or "Kiss Monday." Some boys sprinkled girls with water and started water battles. We were kids being kids.

The Last Days of Summer

World War One memories remained fresh for many Poles. Geographically, Poland covered a large plain in Eastern Europe. The Baltic Sea provided natural defenses on her northern border, and the Carpathian Mountains protected her on the south, but the eastern and western borders had no geographical barriers to discourage invasion. Squeezed between belligerent nations, Poland became a major battleground in World War I. The conflict took the lives of three million men and wounded nine million more. By Armistice Day, (Veteran's Day) November 11, 1918, a third of the Polish people were starving. Battles on farms and farmlands left agricultural lands barren and scorched. Born on November 22, 1902 Daddy was a boy in 1914, but he well remembered the destruction and stench of war.

The map on the following page illustrates Poland's boundaries in 1939.

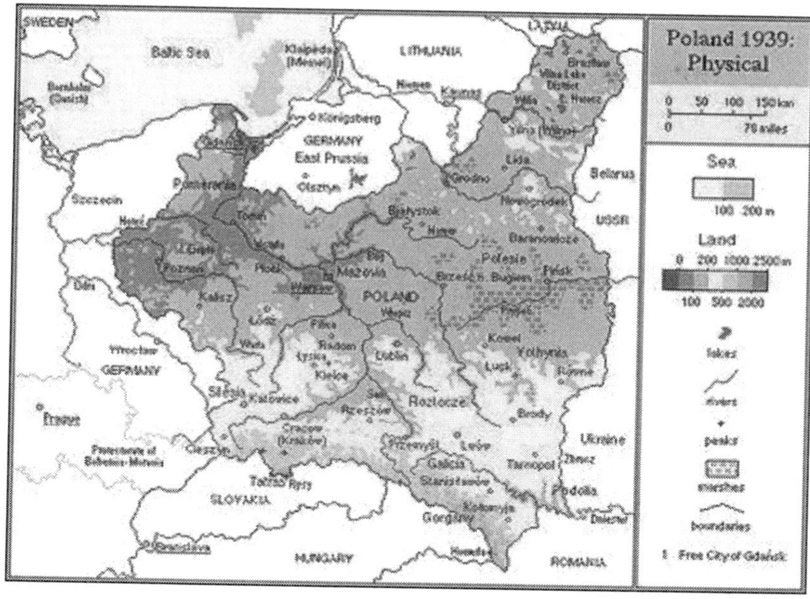

Wikipedia

My father was a very intelligent man. He loved politics and was a natural leader. He saw the threat of War long before the fighting started. My Aunt Janina's house became the central meeting place for the men to discuss rumors and rumblings. Every Sunday, Daddy walked to Aunt Janina's, and he and the other men speculated about Hitler and Nazis plans. Stories and witness accounts came by word of mouth, passed along from family to family, like the children's game of "telephone." Local farmers selling crops in distant markets told what they had seen and heard. Strangers travelling through the village passed on information.

Our parents tried to protect Lodzia and me by not allowing their worry and fear to seep into our daily lives. As sabers rattled, and the invasion drew closer, Lodzia sensed the danger. I was too young to understand. In school, Lodzia listened to whispered conversations among the teachers. She heard rumors and stories from her classmates. She saw the tight lips and sad eyes of our parents, our extended family, and the neighbors. Lodzia finished grade six in the spring of 1939. On the day of the invasion, her teacher disappeared. No one knew what happened to him.

****

Lodzia completed her religious education and received the sacraments at St. Mary's before the invasion. My mother worried I wouldn't get enough religious instruction to be ready for First Communion prior to the War beginning. Everyone realized the future was uncertain. Mom went to the church and talked with Father Karyl, our priest.

She said, "Father, War is coming. I don't think we should wait until Victoria is older to make her first Communion."

Father Karyl agreed, "I'll give you a catechism. You teach her, Helena. When you've finished, come back and Victoria will make her First Communion."

And that's what happened. My mother taught me, and Father Karyl was happy with what I learned. After Mass on a Sunday afternoon, we celebrated my first Holy Communion. My whole family was there, Leocadia, both my grandmothers, aunts, uncles, cousins, and my parents. We had baskets with breads and cheeses and kielbasa. We marked the occasion with a little picnic in the churchyard.

Early in the War, Waffen SS soldiers took Father Karyl to a concentration camp because he opposed the Nazi Regime and Adolph Hitler. I believe he died at Dachau.

Statistics released after the War confirmed 2,720 clerical prisoners at Dachau. Out of that number, 2,579 or nearly ninety-five percent were Roman Catholic.

Prisoners at Dachau celebrate release from captivity on April 29, 1945.

Wikipedia

****

No one could imagine the terror and misery barreling toward us. Few people outside or inside of Germany comprehended Hitler's absolute evil. The fluid border with Ukraine lay a few miles east of Derazno. Months before the German invasion, Ukrainian thugs crossed into the country claiming to be resistance fighters coming to assist Poland if Germany attacked. However, they did not come to help us. They came to pillage the countryside, terrorize, and steal from villagers and farmers. We had no defenses. Derazno didn't have police officers or soldiers to stop the marauding gangs.

For weeks just before dawn, we heard wagons rolling by. My parents ran from the door to the window, watching the Ukrainians.

We prayed they wouldn't stop at our farm, and we prayed for families where they did.

The raiders came to our farm at daybreak waking us from fitful sleep. They stopped their horses and wagons and five of the criminals went to the barn. They took what they wanted from the barn and butchered our cow for its meat. They left the cow's carcass on the barn floor to rot.

I was standing next to my mother in the kitchen, and one of them came crashing through the door demanding salt.

Mom got the salt crock down off its shelf and held it toward him.

"Please, can you leave a couple of tablespoons for us?"

He didn't answer. Instead, he put his gun to her temple. Terrified and screaming, I grabbed her skirt and buried my face in it. Daddy heard the commotion, ran through the door, and saw the guerrilla holding his pistol to my mother's head.

"Helena, give him that salt, please, give him that salt," Daddy said. Mom looked at Daddy with sad eyes and handed the Ukrainian the canister of salt.

Our days were filled with apprehension, and the nights long and fearsome.

Upheaval

On August 25, 1939, Adolph Hitler ordered top echelons of the Nazi party to a high level meeting at Eagles Nest, his hideaway in the Bavarian Mountains.

Hitler told his men the object of war was to destroy the enemy. He ordered his armies to kill all men, women, and children of Polish descent and those who spoke the Polish language. He said War was the only avenue to get the living space Germany needed.

The Third Reich's drive for living space, a policy called *Lebensraum* stemmed from Hitler's conviction that blond-haired, blue-eyed, non-Jewish Caucasians belonged to a master ethnic group he called the Aryan race. He maintained that this "superior race" needed land to expand. Hitler and the National Socialist German Workers Party, (Nazi party) catapulted into power in 1920. Hitler and his coalition declared that "racial superiority" gave Germany the right to dislocate and wipeout entire populations and cultures. According to Hitler, the permanent existence of an ideal, pure white race relied on conquering territory to support its growing population. Hitler advanced his theories of racial superiority on every front. He said people with the finest genetic structure carried Germanic or Nordic genes. Next in descending order came people from the Latin nations: French, Spanish and Italians. On Hitler's scale, Poles registered just above the Jews. Poles would be slave laborers for the Third Reich. He considered us subhuman people, and he planned to exterminate us and erase every trace of our cultures.

****

The Ribbentrop-Molotov pact split Poland into roughly two equal geographical areas. Under the terms of the agreement, Germany annexed western Poland and Ukraine took eastern Poland.

Our peaceful life ended on September 1, 1939 with the German invasion. The military attacks began in the early morning hours of Friday, September 1, 1939 as the Luftwaffe bombed the Polish city of Wieluń. German naval forces launched an attack on the Military Transit Depot in Danzig at the same moment. Fewer than two hundred Poles defended the depot for seven days until it fell to Germany's superior fighting power. In Wieluń, the *Blitzkrieg,* or Lightening War destroyed seventy-five percent of the city on the first day of fighting. Civilian casualties numbered over twelve hundred men, women and children. Sixteen days later, Ukraine forces launched their own offensive on the pretext that Poland "illegally annexed" parts of Ukraine and Byelorussia. They said Ukraine and Russia were coming to the aid of their "blood brothers."

Out-numbered and poorly equipped Poles couldn't halt the rapid military advances. The last battle took place near the little town of Kock, in central eastern Poland just a few kilometers north of the Wieprz River. By October 6, 1939, our nation had fallen, and we found ourselves squeezed once more between two powerful aggressors, Germany and Russia. Poland's bad dream became a nightmare.

The Waffen-SS and their paramilitary group called *Einsatzgruppen* occupied every city, town and village in a few days. Warsaw lay in ruins. Wilno lay in ashes. Nazis with overwhelming military strength under their command rolled into Derewno and Derazno. Heinrich Himmler was their commanding officer. His orders to the Waffen-SS and the paramilitary units were simple and clear: Terrorize, brutalize and murder Poles.

****

My mother made frequent trips to the market in Derewno to sell linens, eggs and cheeses. On a mild, warm day in mid-September, she heard the air fill with curses, shouts and screams in Polish, Yiddish and German. Jackboots with iron heels and hobnailed soles hammered the street. Shoppers and storekeepers slipped outdoors to see the commotion and stood in shocked silence as Nazis using brute force herded forty or fifty people toward the edge of town. Men, women, the elderly, young boys and girls, mothers carrying babies and small children, even the Rabbi were beaten, battered, and shoved through the streets. Shovels waited for them at a pre-selected site. Using rifle butts and bayonets soldiers forced the Jews to dig. When the trench was deep and wide, they pushed, shoved, and rammed the Jews into the pit. Human beings were pleading and crying as soldiers emptied their rifles into the families they condemned to death. Nazis snatched babies and children, knocked their heads together, and threw them in with the bodies. In a few minutes, everyone in the grave lay dead or dying. A deep silence fell over the witnesses. The executioners lit cigarettes and strolled away. Stunned, the bystanders crept back into town. My mother, numb with fear did not remember walking home. I have no words to describe how frightened and upset she was. Sometimes during dark sleepless nights, I remember her sobs, "My God! You wouldn't believe what they're doing to the people there."

The occupiers' utter brutality and cold-bloodedness haunted her until she went to her grave.

It didn't take long for news of Nazi murders and brutalities to spread. Himmler's death squads marched into towns, and rounded up all the men and teenage boys. They barricaded them into barns and set the structures ablaze. Anyone who tried to escape the fire was shot. When they came to Derazno, Waffen-SS troops arrested the village men and boys and locked them in my uncle's barn. Derazno's women gathered eggs, hams, cheeses, butter, and offered the food to the commanding officer in an attempt to gain the men's freedom. He took the bribe and ordered the men and boys be freed. The doors opened and the men and boys bolted in every direction. They feared they would be killed running from the barn.

Three days later, a squad of armed Wehrmacht thundered onto our farm riding motorcycles. One shouted in Polish, "You are being evacuated. Pack your wagon with enough supplies for two days. Be ready to leave this afternoon."

The Polish speaker got back on his motorcycle, and they roared off to spread the order to the rest of Derazno.

Later that afternoon, soldiers came to evacuate us. If we refused to go, we would be shot. I was young and afraid, but I trusted my parents to keep me safe.

Mom put hard cheese, bread, a little flour and a small piece of bacon in a sack she tied around her waist. She hid the cache by wearing a sweater over her dress. Daddy packed tools, a few articles of clothing, and four blankets into the wagon.

It was a tragedy, not just for us personally, but for the entire country. We left everything behind my parents worked decades to accomplish. Even more tragic we lost our freedom. When soldiers came that afternoon, Daddy hitched the horses to our wagon, and we fell into line with the rest of our family and neighbors. Nazi soldiers on horseback rode alongside us. The whole family – my uncles, aunts, and cousins left the village at the same time. Everyone that is, except eighty-year-old Grandmother Maria Wilniewicz, my mother's mother. She refused to leave.

"You go. I am not going with you. I'm not taking my old bones no place. I'm old. Let them do whatever they want to with me. I'm not leaving here."

Her sons, her daughters and her grandchildren pleaded and begged her to come with us. She told those who tried to convince her, "Leave me in peace."

The SS ordered us to move out and urged the horses and wagons forward, using their rifle butts. We had no choice. I watched Grandmother Maria slip away into the cornfield. It was the last time I saw her alive.

After the War, my cousin Joseph, Aunt Janinia's oldest son, went back to Derazno. Nothing remained of the village except ashes and burnt timbers. Weeds and brush overgrew the fields. Small trees had taken root where my mother's flax had once thrived.

"I smelled death in that place," Joseph said.

At Grandmother's house, Joseph found her charred remains. Her Rosary lay in the ashes between the stove and small window where she often sat. Joseph gathered up her bones, took them to the village cemetery, and buried her. I hope they killed her before they burned down her house.

****

The first night, we stopped in a meadow not far from St. Mary's Church. Horses and wagons continued to pull in until the early morning hours. No one got much sleep.

A recurring rumor circulated among the Poles saying we were going to the train depot at Stolpce.

Three days later, we camped in a soccer stadium in the center of that small city. Soldiers sped by in motorized vehicles splashing mud, shouting, "Unload your wagons." I remember little of the trip to Stolpce except it poured rain the whole way.

Mom and Daddy emptied the wagon. We stood on the muddy soccer field with our belongings heaped around our feet. Two soldiers dressed in gray-green field uniforms drove the horses and wagon away. We never saw Kara and Kasztanka, again.

The guards paid little attention to us that night. We heard their laughter floating over the breeze. Burning cigarette ends resembled fireflies blinking in the distance. It was dark and moonless when Daddy and eight other men held a furtive meeting. They devised a plan to escape and go back to their homes and farms in Poland. Daddy agreed that we would go with them. When everything was quiet, the escapees picked up their bundles of food and clothing and disappeared into the night. There were sixteen adults and several children. The risk was great. If caught we would be shot, no questions asked. We regrouped and rested in the shadows of a large church. My legs were tired from running. Mom was breathing hard. Leocadia's face was red from exertion. Daddy held us tight. We had escaped. But, now what? I overheard my father and mother talking.

"Why are we running, Helena? Where are we going? We have no home. I have no horses, and no animals. We do not have anything. Where are we going to live? We should go wherever the Germans take us. It is all we can do. We have nothing left in Poland."

Mom listened and agreed. Before sunrise, we walked back to our spot in the field.

Some of the escapees decided to take their chances and make the trip back to Poland. Survivors would face starvation and the bitter cold of Polish winters. We learned later that every Pole lived a grim existence first under German occupation, and then under Communism.

That afternoon soldiers marched us to the train depot.

The same guards who saw no one escape during the night jammed us into freight cars in the morning. Soldiers screamed *Schnell! Schnell*, hurry, hurry.

Poor souls who didn't move fast enough were slammed by gun butts and jabbed with bayonets. Bodies packed in around me in that boxcar. I grabbed Daddy's pant leg terrified of losing him. People elbowed, jostled, and jockeyed for space. Children screamed. Men and women pleaded with indifferent soldiers who ignored them. The train pulled away from the station, and we began the long, wretched journey to north central Germany. Bodies filled every inch of space. The air grew stifling. Young children pooped where they stood, even adults couldn't hold back the urge and urinated. The stench made me sick to my stomach. I cannot describe the train trip. It was so brutal and sadistic I do not have enough words to express it. The human contempt showered on us on that train was evil in its purest form.

****

The swill our pigs ate was better than the weak and watery slop given to us on the train. Thank God, my mother smuggled bread and cheese. She insisted I eat in that cattle car even though the mere thoughts of food made my stomach turn.

When the steam engine stopped to reload coal, we ran into the woods to relieve ourselves. Some tried to escape, and the brat-a-tat, brat-a-tat barking of machine gun fire thundered. After sunset, a few men and women tried to escape by jumping off the slow moving train. Nevertheless, no one escaped the firing squads. Nothing interfered with the journey west.

People perished on the train and Waffen-SS dumped their bodies from the boxcar onto the sides of the railroad tracks.

One night on the trip to Stolpce my father's younger brother, Alexander, disappeared. My parents and his family grieved for him until at last they concluded he was dead. What happened to Alexander will always remain a mystery. Like the mysteries about so many other people who went missing. The train trip ended at Magdeburg, Germany. There some SS troops emptied the boxcars the same way they loaded us in Stolpce. They used guns, bayonets, and brute force. We staggered off the train dazed and confused, blinking in the bright sun. Soldiers hurled curses at us pushing us into jagged columns. When I close my eyes, I still hear the harsh shouted orders. Our guards seemed to think that if they yelled and screamed loud enough we would suddenly understand German.

We stumbled through the town to a detention camp. At the camp entrance, soldiers separated us into two columns. One long line for men, another for women. Older Poles wore worried, resigned faces. Soldiers marched the men away over a slight rise, and we lost sight of them. As Daddy disappeared my mother's face became ashen. A few men and boys resisted, but any sign of rebellion resulted in a vicious beating or a bullet to the head.

Our line was a miserable collection of women, mothers with babies and small children, teenage girls, old women, and little girls. The three of us held hands as our column snaked forward to a makeshift building equipped with showers. Nazis shaved the heads of some of the women in line. I still don't know why they didn't shave us all. I wondered how I would look with no hair. When it was our turn for the showers, we took off our dresses and put them atop a growing pile. Together, Mom and I went under the frigid, stinging, stinking water. Lodzia was next in line behind us. The overwhelming smell of chemicals saturated the air. It was hard to breath and my empty stomach churned. I had no clothes when I got out, but I still wore my shoes. A large middle-aged woman wearing a shapeless brown uniform with a bright red swastika armband tossed me a light summer dress. She wasn't smiling. Soldiers herded us back to the camp entrance. Several guards harried the men along toward us. We held our breath until we saw Daddy coming back. He was next to the last in the long line of men and boys.

After the showers, and the men and women were reunited, they locked us in a drafty barn under the vigilant eyes of the SS. The guards permitted limited outhouse breaks and gave us a cup of thin soup twice a day. We could have escaped from the rickety barn, but the Nazis armed with Mauser bolt-action rifles would have used us for target practice. We were deep in Germany with no place to run or hide. Wooden bunks, stacked four high, with thin, stained mattresses filled the space. We had no blankets. I slept fitfully on a bunk curled up next to my mother. Everything smelled of strong chemicals and sweat. Fear reigned. I clung to my mother.

Using gun butts and body language, they drove a dozen families, including ours, out through the double barn doors. All the other Poles remained in the barn. Driven like cattle, we walked back to the depot and boarded a passenger train. This car had seats. The train pulled out of the station and headed northwest. A few hours later the train stopped at the village of Horst, Germany. Soldiers prodded us off the train. This was our final destination. The train whistle sounded three times and pulled away from the depot. All the other Poles, our relatives and friends, continued east with the train.

LIFE WITH THE GERMANS

A local farmer, Eric Jahnke, met us on the platform and we walked to his farm. Jahnke was a giant of a man, built like an American football player. He stood over six feet tall. His wife, Frau Jahnke was a squat, round, middle-aged woman with frizzled flaxen hair, and no smile on her face.

The Jahnke's gave us a small outbuilding to live in. Frau Jahnke handed us woolen blankets to use on hard sleeping pallets. We had no heat for warmth nor stove for cooking. Frau Jahnke prepared all the food and distributed each person's meager rations. My parents and my sister worked long hours in the fields on the Jahnke farm. Too young to work, I stayed in the outbuilding or roamed the farm all day. I missed my father, playing with my sister, and especially my mother. As the youngest family member, I had been the family's darling, now I spent the days alone.

A disabled veteran of World War I lived in the shed near us. An amputation from just below his left knee kept him limping along on crutches although his disability didn't slow him down. He was a slight man, with deep pockmarks on his face. I never saw him without a cigarette dangling from one corner of his mouth. He reminded me of a fox because his movements were twitchy and quick. He worked at odd jobs around the farm, and at night, he locked the Russian prisoners of war into a barbed wire enclosed barn. I was afraid of him.

****

Jahnke knew everything, our names, birthdays, and even the Polish village we came from. The Nazi Immigration Office kept accurate records on every foreigner who entered Germany. After the War, at the Nuremburg Trials these precise, detailed records helped bring Nazi War criminals to justice.

I heard Frau Jahnke calling my name while I was sitting under a leafy tree playing with some sticks. I dawdled across the yard toward her afraid I had done something wrong. Frau Jahnke spoke to me in a gentle voice, and gave me a charming little purse. It was made of creamy tweed fabric and lined with beautiful emerald green satin. The gift was an unexpected act of kindness and a lovely surprise for a little girl who didn't know it was her birthday.

We stayed at the Jahnke farm for a few weeks. By the end of August, the light summer dress I wore wasn't warm enough. A bright afternoon sun warmed the daylight hours, but after sunset temperatures plummeted. On a crisp fall day, Mrs. Jahnke went to Nazi officials in Horst and told them she didn't have room for our family. She said, "They can't stay in the shed where they live now. It doesn't have a stove for heating, and they'll freeze to death. We don't have another place with heat where we can move them."

Herr Jahnke told Daddy about his wife's conversation. In a few days, soldiers took us back to the train depot in Horst. We didn't know our destination. Moreover, my parents had overheard whispered rumors of special work camps for Jews and Poles. The train headed south and stopped in the village of Modessa. Farmer Erich Gruber met us at the whistle stop. Three Waffen SS stood next to him. The soldiers waited for Lodzia to detrain and grabbed her by the arm. My mother stifled a scream. I thought she would faint. Lodzia stumbled, and a soldier caught her. Lodzia's face was gray. Fear gripped us. My father shouted at the soldiers "What are you doing? She is a child. Let her go, she belongs with us!"

One of the SS soldiers who spoke Polish put his hands on my father's shoulders and stopped him from doing anything rash.

"Calm down! Calm down! Your daughter will live with old people who need help. She'll be all right. They live near the farm where you are going."

My parents were helpless. They knew you did not argue with Nazi soldiers, and live to tell about it. Anger and frustration showed on my father's face. Lodzia turned and waved back as the Waffen SS walked her to a large black car with Swastikas emblazoned on its doors.

****

On the Gruber farm, we had half a house to live in. A German family lived next door, but they didn't associate with us. We had one large room, and two smaller rooms. The stove kept the bigger room warm. After work, Mom brought branches and pieces of wood and kept the stove burning. The water well was across the road. It was easier to bring in water for drinking and washing than it had been at Jahnke farm. The outhouse was located behind the house. While our living conditions improved over those on the Jahnke farm, they were still meager. There was no comparison with what we had left behind in Derazno.

We were forbidden to leave Modessa, and there was no Catholic Church in the village. In fact, the village had no churches at all. In the years we worked for the Germans we didn't see a priest or attend mass.

****

My mother and father left for the fields at dawn and I stayed alone. On nice days, I wandered through the orchards and barns, or watched my parents working. Otherwise, I went to Gruber's house and helped the German novices. In those days, young girls apprenticed with families to learn the proper ways to cook, clean, and keep house. After a training period, the girls went home and married.

Nineteen-year-old Hannah and twenty-year-old Anna were kind to me. Their parents sent them to live with the Gruber's to learn housekeeping essentials from Frau Gruber. I didn't feel so lonely when doing little chores with them. I peeled potatoes, washed the dishes, or swept the front steps. Laundry took one entire day spent in a hot, steamy washroom. The girls heated water for the wringer washer and hung the clothes outside to dry. Too young to help, I watched from the sidelines. Mom worked with the girls on laundry day. With the Gruber family laundry finished, Mom washed our clothes and bedding.

When they were able, the German girls kept a small slice of cake or a serving of pudding for me. They had to hide the treat from Frau Gruber or she gave them a tongue-lashing. Frau was a dedicated Nazi committed to Hitler's philosophy of racial superiority and German entitlement. Her husband, Erich was not as devoted to the cause, but he didn't object to using slave labor provided by the Nazi regime.

****

We ate our rations in a storage space off the kitchen of Gruber's house. My family, another Polish worker, a Serb, a Swiss herdsman, and two women - a Russian and a Pole - sat at an old, but sturdy, round oak table. The Grubers didn't eat with us. The German girls served them in their dining room, and the girls ate in the kitchen. As at the Jahnke's, Frau Gruber cooked for everyone.

Thin, watery soups were standard fare. Sometimes the soup was so thin Mom cried, "This is more like water than soup." If we didn't have bland, tasteless soup, we had eggs. I remember a pancake cut in slices like a pizza, and each of us got one small slice. We had meat and potatoes once during the years we spent on Gruber's farm. Eric killed three rabbits in his field and Frau cooked them for Sunday dinner. I looked forward to Sunday afternoons when Frau baked a *zucker kuchen* or sugar cake. It was a simple flat yeast cake sprinkled with sugar. My parents got small slices, and I ate the rest.

****

Besides Gruber's substantial farm, the community of Modessa supported one other large farm and a few smaller holdings. The center of the village had a modest butcher shop, a small post office, a Gestapo outpost and a small medical clinic. A widowed German woman managed the post office from the front of her house, and she ran a small segregated bar on the second floor. She was raising a son. We often saw Herr Gruber walking to the bar in the evening. We never saw him going home.

It is a mystery how my mother knew her sister's family was in Braunschweig. Allies began aerial bombings of German industrial centers in 1940. British bombers attacked German factories at night, and after America entered the War, bombs fell during the day. Forced laborers, most of them Polish, who survived the bombing raids often died of starvation or from over work.

We had no stove in our quarters for cooking and Mother still had a small amount of flour and bacon left from the exodus from Poland.

Determined to send the food to her sister, she made up a parcel and took it to Modessa's post office. The postmistress saw her coming, saw the parcel in her hand, and gasped. A German trooper could walk in and arrest them both.

She called Erich Gruber, "Mrs. Sielicki is here with a package. She wants to mail it to Braunschweig."

Farmer Gruber heard the fear in the woman's voice. He got on his bicycle and pedaled to the post office. Towering over my mother he asked, "Helena, what's in that package? Who is it for? Where are you sending it?"

My mother stood her ground and looked up into his eyes, "Herr Gruber, my family is suffering in Braunschweig. They work in the factories. I have a little flour and bacon from Poland and I want to help them, so I am to sending it to them."

Gruber turned toward the door and shouted over his shoulder to the postmistress.

"Send it."

Gruber got on his bicycle and went back toward the farm. I never knew if my aunt got the parcel. I think Erich Gruber was a decent man trapped in the insanity of Hitler's Germany. However, he accepted the free slave laborers he was sent.

****

Mom found a chipped cup in a corner of a barn. She washed it and checked for leaks. When she milked the cows, she squeezed a little of it into the cup. Mom was very thin. Her collarbones peeked out from the neckline of the faded, loose dress she wore. I knew later that she gave me the milk she pilfered, her Sunday sugar cake, and most of her food rations.

During the winter months, when the fields were fallow, Daddy worked in the barns repairing tools. Mom looked after livestock and worked for Frau Gruber. The workers prepared the extensive fields and gardens for spring plantings. My father chopped and stacked firewood. My parents worked long days.

****

The three Gruber children were the only children I knew. Manfrit was thirteen; Helga and I were both eight. The youngest girl, Erica was five. I called them ugly Polish words that they didn't understand.

My favorite bad name *gówno szwaby* or pig shit. My eight-year-old vocabulary wasn't large enough to express my feelings of anger and frustration, but I did my best.

Two other Polish families came to Modessa. I longed for children I could talk with; Polish speaking playmates, so I went to say hello. Both families had taken the German oath of allegiance, and neither family wanted anything to do with me. The children went inside when they saw me coming.

I didn't understand. Upset I cried all the way back to Grubers.

Daddy said, "Those kids are afraid to play with you." Then I understood.

Conscripted foreign workers who renounced their citizenship and swore allegiance to Germany and the Third Reich received special privileges, better treatment and their children went to school. My father was proud to be Polish. He refused to abandon his country, and he refused to swear allegiance to Hitler. I didn't go to school.

A small pond lay behind Gruber's house that froze over in early winter. It wasn't smooth ice but it made a good skating rink. The Gruber kids had leather ice skates with sharp blades. I didn't. My wooden shoes, called *sabots*, turned out to be better suited for skating across the frozen pond than the Gruber kids' fancy skates. I knew Manfrit wanted to skate faster than me, and he thought if he had wooden shoes like mine, he could beat me.

"Look how fast Victoria flies across the ice! Mom and Dad, I want shoes like Victoria," Manfrit told his parents.

****

Lodzia worked for an aging couple in Modessa. She had her own bed, and she could bathe in their tub. They shared food rations with her. She did the housework, helped with meals, and worked in the gardens. Lodzia was safe. As an adult, I learned what happened to many young girls from rural Polish communities under the German occupation. The aging couple lived near the Gruber farm so I often walked over to visit. The twosome got used to seeing me and knew Lodzia was my sister, so I was always welcome. I became the information conduit between Lodzia, Mom and Daddy.

****

On Christmas 1941, Lodzia gave me pants and jacket cut down from a woman's blue woolen dress. The German hausfrau Lodzia worked for gave her the heavy wool and helped her sew the outfit. With Germany on a war footing austerity ruled the marketplace. Frau Gruber gave me cast-offs and hand-me-downs from her children, but the clothing was often one season late. So I'd get summer clothes in late fall and winter clothes in the spring.

In Poland, we had the same standard of living ordinary Germans had. Now on the Gruber and Jahnke farms, my parents trudged back exhausted and dirty from the fields. In payment for their labor, we received scarcely enough food to stay alive. Many Germans looked on Poles as disposable, sub-humans to be tolerated as long as they advanced the goals of the Third Reich.

****

Farmer Gruber owned acres of flourishing pastures, fields, and orchards. A medium-sized pear tree grew near the edge of one of his orchards. Delicate white pear blossoms covered the tree in the spring welcoming the sun and warmer days. The falling petals reminded me of fragile snowflakes. Bosc pears matured from small green orbs to sweet smelling ripe fruit over the summer. By mid-October, overripe or damaged pears dropped from the tree. When that happened I scooped them up, ate my fill, and took what I could carry to my mother. The smell of ripening pears still reminds me of those golden, sweet, bruised pieces of fruit, of how good they tasted, and how they filled my empty stomach.

Some summers Erich's parents came to visit. Family and workers called Erich's father Opa. Erich's mother, Oma, had a physical disability that kept her indoors. Sometimes I saw her watching us out of a third story window, but she never came out of the house.

Opa was a gentle, distinguished man with steel grey hair combed slick straight back over his head. He told me he was a veteran of the First World War while we worked companionably in the garden. Erich, who was taller than average towered over him. Opa's shoulders stooped from advancing age. He smiled often and his words were kind. His soft-spoken speech softened the harsh, guttural sounds of the German language. He taught me to speak a little German as we moved along the rows weeding and hoeing or plucking produce. When we finished for the day, he always gave me a little treat. Sometimes a few strawberries or an apple, and his gifts were always welcome. Watching them pack Gruber's truck to leave the farm left me feeling sad and lonely. I hoped they would come to visit again soon.

****

On a Christmas Eve I remember, Daddy went into the woods and cut the tip off a small pine tree. He made a hook from scrap metal and used it to hang our tree. The lovely smell of freshly cut pine drifted through our rooms. The Gruber kids gave me a little crepe paper and I made decorations. Ornaments were pinecones and treasures I found in the woods. Christmas was a regular day, and Gruber made no mention of the holiday. Daddy read the nativity story aloud. We couldn't help but remember the Christmases we celebrated in Poland. However, the little pine tree made Christmas memorable that year.

Erich Gruber grew sugar beets the size of small watermelons. He sold his crop to a sugar processer in Peine. Gruber grew wheat and hay, but the beets brought in the majority of the farm's Reichsmarks

I always knew where to find Mom. She made a point of telling me where she would be working on the farm if I needed her.

One day, near lunchtime I went to help the girls. It was later in the morning than usual because I slept late. Frau Gruber had grown accustomed to seeing me in the kitchen early in the morning. That day, she stormed into the kitchen taking me to task in her shrill voice, "Where have you been? You should have been here a long time ago! You are late for your work!"

Surprised and bewildered I tried to tell her I overslept. Frau Gruber pulled back her hand and slapped me hard across my face. An ugly red welt rose on my cheek. Crying and running out the door, I ran to my mother. I was still sobbing when I got to her. She dropped her hoe, knelt on the ground and put her arms around me.

"What's wrong? What happened?"

I told her between hiccups and tears, "Frau slapped me."

She held me tighter and kissed my swollen cheek. She wiped my face with the hem of her dress. Dirt mixed with tears smudged my cheeks. She took me by my hand and we stumbled toward our quarters.

My mother was so furious red splotches bloomed on her cheeks. I had never seen my mother so angry!

My gentle, down-to-earth mother yelled, "Her children are in school! You are not supposed to work! You're not fourteen years old! You're still a child! There must be a law against Frau Gruber hitting you."

When we got to our quarters, she washed my hands and face with a soft rag, all the time muttering about the injustice of slapping a child. She looked at me with sad eyes and announced, "We're going to Peine and we will make certain she never, ever touches you again! There must be laws to protect you. We will find someone in charge."

My determined mother said we would walk the two kilometers to Peine even though we were forbidden to leave the village. Farmer Erich saw us walking down the road from his vantage point in the beet field. He went into the house and questioned the German girls. Hannah told him "Frau Gruber slapped Victoria." Our farmer got his bicycle from the barn and peddled after us. It didn't take him long to catch up.

"Helena, where are you going?"

"To report your wife to the police! She slapped my child. Your children are in school! My daughter should be in school. She is not supposed to work, she is too young! She helps the girls at the house because she is lonely. Victoria should be in school with your children!"

Herr Gruber heard my mothers' raised voice, saw her flushed face and saw her hands shaking with fury.

"Helena go back home and stay with your daughter today. I'm sorry this happened! I will take care of it. It will never happen again."

And it is true. She never hit me again.

When her daughter, Erica, came home from school with lice one day, I was the one Frau Gruber blamed. Frau grabbed me by my arm and jerked me into a side room. She tugged on my hair and yanked me around searching for vermin on my scalp. She found nothing. It was like another slap in the face. She treated me as if I was — as if I was filth. We had a tub, and we bathed often. Mom washed my hair. We were clean. After the lice incident, Frau Gruber ignored me altogether. When she gave her children treats, of hard candy or cookies, she passed me by as though I did not exist.

Frau Gruber was a true Nazi convert. She was bad. Bad. Bad. Bad.

****

The Third Reich took thousands of Polish prisoners of War, and thousands of conscripted laborers to support the German War machine. They worked hard in factories during the day and spent the nights in guarded barracks surrounded by barbed wire. They were always hungry and exhausted. It was curious. Some POWs interned near Gruber's farm could leave for a few hours on random Sunday afternoons. The rules were be back by curfew or be shot. But, really, where could Polish boys escape to from the middle of Germany? They didn't speak German, and they had no money. They were simple farm boys like my cousins. Three or four of the POW's often walked or rode bicycles to the Gruber farm and spent their free time talking with my father. It was good to hear Polish being spoken.

I loved it when I saw those boys bicycling down the road. One of them always let me ride his bike. It didn't matter it was a boy's bike, and I had to twist and turn and stretch to reach the pedals. I learned to ride a two-wheeled bike. I had lots of skinned knees and scratched elbows learning to balance, but I had a ball riding a bicycle.

When the POWs came to see my Father, they always had War news, and carried with them Polish newspapers and leaflets.

Until their visits, we heard nothing except German War propaganda. Berlin's news sources reported Germany winning battle after battle. For most of the War, we believed, along with most Germans citizens, the lies and propaganda spewing from Berlin.

Lodzia heard whispered conversations and idle talk about how the War was progressing. She told me, and I repeated what she said to Mom and Daddy. We didn't have a radio or access to outside news until the boys brought news from the Resistance. The Polish papers talked about Allied Air Force bombings and successful sabotage forays that disrupted rail travel, internal communications, and destruction of strategic bridges. Rumors of an Allied invasion became more insistent. Daddy read the Polish papers, pamphlets and leaflets from cover to cover. We saw countless Allied planes flying overhead. But it was the news we got from the boys that raised our spirits. As the War drew to a close, German soldiers and citizens understood that Germany was losing, and harsh German attitudes toward us softened somewhat.

****

The Kotwika at left was the flag of the Polish Resistance movement. Designed by Anna Smoleńska. Arrested by the Gestapo in November 1942, she died in Auschwitz in March 1943. She was 23 years old.

Wikipedia

****

With no work in the fields on Sundays, it was the day Daddy taught me to read, write, and work simple arithmetic problems. The Gruber kids gave me paper and a pencil and I practiced writing. I learned to read from a New Testament Daddy smuggled out of Poland.

****

One day the sky was blue with just a few marshmallow clouds. Mom and Daddy were working in the beet fields, and I was helping the girls by peeling potatoes. Without warning, the incessant drone of planes broke through the rattle and clatter of morning chores. Frau, the girls and I went outside to look at the sky. Scores of giant monster planes, sunlight glancing off their wings, lumbered over the horizon. The air shimmered in the heat. Heavy, burdened bombers flew over our heads. An angry hive of small, agile Luftwaffe fighter planes appeared out of the sun, guns roaring. The fighters danced and crisscrossed across the sky attacking the bombers. Fascinated, we stood out in the open and watched the aerial ballet. A bomber with smoke and flames erupting from its wings fell from the sky. The fighters screaming engines hurt my ears. My neck ached from looking up, and the acidic smell of cordite took my breath. Smoke from combat turned the sky dirty gray. The unescorted, lumbering bombers could not dodge the lightning-fast Luftwaffe fighter planes. Bullets flew everywhere. Gunfire peppering the ground broke the spell. My heart thumped in my chest, and adrenalin powered my feet. Screaming and crying I raced to find my mother. She called my name and ran toward me. She grabbed my hand and we raced toward our quarters. Bullets came at us faster and closer, some missing us by mere inches, spraying the surrounding earth. We ran through the open beet field. There was no shelter. Mom and I were running and out of breath. I stumbled and we dropped to the ground. Bullets from the dueling planes hit the ground just missing us. "Lay down!" Mom shouted, and she covered me with her body. Our faces were in the dirt. I couldn't breathe. I thought she would squeeze me to death.

Mom prayed, "Hail Mary, full of grace, the Lord is with Thee." The feisty, agile German fighters forced the unwieldy bombers to turn back. As the big planes retreated, they dropped their bombs on the countryside surrounding Modessa. Bombs fell in Farmer Gruber's fields leaving gaping craters where beets once grew. The bombers flew west and out of sight. Unhurt but terrified, Mom and I ran toward to the relative safety of our quarters.

After the bombing men from Modessa and the surrounding farms cleared the beet field. It was a dangerous job done under the threat of exploding ammunition.

A few weeks later, Stas, a Polish man who worked for Gruber, came to our quarters to show off a shell he found in the beet field. It was night and Mom and I were asleep in the little alcove off the living area. "Let's see what's inside," Stas pried the outer casing off using a hammer and chisel. Without warning, the shell exploded. A deafening roar went up. Stas's leg and knee shattered and blood ran from his wound.

Mom and I thought a bomb hit the house. Ready to run we stopped in the doorway and watched my father tying a rag tourniquet high on Stas's thigh.

Hearing the explosion, Erich Gruber and two men came running. They took the injured man outside.

"Quick take Stas to the clinic," Gruber shouted, "Hurry, hurry! He's losing a lot of blood."

With the immediate crisis over, Erich Gruber exploded.

"Adolf! How did you let this happen? Why did you let him take a shell apart in here? Your little girl and your wife were sleeping in there! You sat next to him. It's amazing the whole place didn't blow up with all of you in it." Daddy was in shock. Erich was yelling that it was a wonder we were still alive. Daddy knew Erich was right. It was a miracle we were not all killed. Daddy had minor cuts on his hands and face, and he could not hear for days afterward unless we shouted. His hearing was never quite the same after that incident.

****

Over the days and weeks, we saw greater numbers of Allied planes. Scores of American B-24 Liberator bombers flew over us. Smoke from fires and explosions turned the day sky to night over

Braunschweig. We stood outside and watched planes drop their payloads on the horizon.

Thank you Lord! Maybe someday we will be free.

As a child I thought when the War was over we would return to the comfortable lifestyle we had before. On restless nights, I dream about my family and the terrible years between 1939 and 1945. The anguish my parents felt when Nazis forced them off their land was devastating and heartbreaking. For generations Poles raised families and continued farming through centuries of wars and shifting political borders. They lived off the land through the political partitions imposed by Russia, Austria, and Germany. The Polish people endured all the various governments that came and went throughout the centuries.

They survived the madness and carnage of World War I, and then came the slaughter and bloodshed of World War II. Polish citizens were left with nothing not even their own souls. Can you imagine how anyone gets through that? How do you leave everything, not knowing where you are going, and fearing for your family and your life? Not knowing if you will live to see your children grown? When I was young, I didn't understand. I am older now, and when the memories come haunting, I am crushed with grief and loss.

****

After Germany surrendered on Monday, May 7, 1945, we stayed on Gruber's farm for several days. Lodzia heard the news on German radio the next day, and ran to tell us. We were overjoyed. In August 1945, I turned eleven

Daddy offered a prayer of gratitude. "Thank you Lord, You have made us free."

Before many days passed, Americans soldiers reached Modessa and Gruber's farm. Two of the GIs spoke broken American Polish.

My father and the GIs spent hours talking. The combat hardened Americans told us, "Take anything you want from the Grubers. Just get it. Take it."

"I want nothing from them. I want nothing," my father said.

With the War over, my sister came back to us to stay. We were together as a family for the first time in nearly six years. The Grubers continued to provide meals for us, and my father, because he was a good man, worked in the fields for a few more days.

That was our life in Germany during the War.

LIMBO

With the hostilities ended, and the armistice signed, Ukraine finished swallowing Eastern Poland including Derazno and Derewno. Political powers shifted Poland's border further west to accommodate the Russian ultimatum of control of Eastern Poland. My family's personal nightmare within wartime Germany ended. Now, new and different challenges confronted us. Where would we go? What would we do? Living under Communism was unthinkable to my parents. We would not return to Poland.

Aunt Amelia sent her son, Henry, to the Gruber farm to tell us of the displaced persons camp in Braunschweig about twenty kilometers away. When this grown up cousin arrived, he didn't resemble the cousin I remembered at all. Henry was no longer a boy but a world-weary man. He made bombs in a munitions factory in Braunschweig for the duration of the War. He spoke quietly about friends and relatives who died of starvation, disease, and exhaustion. Henry was lucky to be alive, and he often wondered why he had lived when so many others did not. The young Henry, I remembered, was tall and thin but not skinny. He loved to laugh, and he liked to tease me. The older scrawny, solemn cousin of mine seldom smiled, and he never laughed. Henry's scalp peeked out from clumps of thinning brown hair, and his head was too big for his body. Henry's ragged shirt displayed a purple patch with the letter "P." Curious, I asked him, "What's that patch mean, Henry?"

Henry told me, "The letter told Germans we were Poles. We had to sew the badges on our clothes and wear them. If you were caught without the patch, you could be shot. The Jews sewed a yellow six - pointed star on their clothing. Wearing that emblem was a death sentence for the Jews and the "P" was often a death sentence for Poles. Modessa was small. Everyone knew the Poles in Modessa, so we never had to sew the patch on our clothing.

Henry said, "Two soldiers gave me a ride in their Jeep part of the way here. I told them I was trying to locate relatives."

"How did your mother and dad find us?" Daddy asked.

Henry sat down on the step. "Mom didn't tell me how she knew. The British Military has opened a camp for refugees. We live in a room in one of the German officer's barracks. We have food, and they gave us clothing and household goods. Doctors and nurses take care of sick people. We have a priest and a church, and the school goes up to grade six. My parents are there, and my Uncle's family, too. Some of my aunts, uncles and cousins are there now. I saw a few of our Derazno neighbors. You should come to the camp. You'll be safe there."

My father listened and nodded. He was not one to make sudden decisions, so his quick answer surprised us.

"Helena, we will go to the camp. Poland is gone; it belongs to Ukraine. We won't go back there."

****

A few days later, my sister, Henry and I walked to Braunschweig. Lodzia and I stayed with Henry's parents and waited for Mom and Daddy to arrive. Back at Gruber's, my father spoke to Erich, "I want to take my family to the camp in Braunschweig. You will drive us there in your truck. We'll take the table, the two benches and the beds."

Erich panicked, "I can't! I can't go to Braunschweig. They'll kill me!" My father's eyes hardened, "Yes, Eric you will drive us! Don't worry. Nobody will hurt you. I'll make sure nobody touches you."

Gruber looked at my father and saw the determination on his face. Mom, Dad and Erich loaded the furniture onto his truck and drove to Braunschweig. No one harmed or threatened Gruber.

World War II shifted and dislodged millions of people. Food, shelter, and medicine were scarce all over Europe. In October 1945 the camps originally operated by the International Relief Organization, or IRO, became the responsibility of the United Nations Relief and Rehabilitation Administration. Crates, barrels, and boxes arrived stamped with the acronym "UNRRA." Decades passed before I learned what UNRRA meant.

New refugees arrived at Braunschweig every day. Many still wore the hated purple "P" identifying them as Poles.

We arrived at the camp and our living assignment was a building on Braunschweig Strasse. Five families lived in the same place. We didn't have running water or bathing facilities and the building itself was in poor condition. It was cold and drafty, and rainwater trickled through holes in the roof. German infantrymen, many of them draftees, lived in the barracks during the War.

Two weeks later, military personnel moved all five families to a much nicer building on Broizemer Strasse. The stark building housed German officers during the hostilities. We were the last families to live in the Braunschweig Strasse barracks. Each of the Broizemer Strasse barracks contained thirty rooms, ten on each floor. Each floor held washrooms with shower stalls, sinks and toilets. No bathtubs to my disappointment. Every family had one room in the former Waffen-SS officers' quarters. The rooms were small; a table, two benches and two beds filled the space. The walls were painted military grey. Mom cooked on a one-burner hot plate. We had running water, which we'd never had before, a sink, a closet and a window. On sunny days, light and shadow shining through the window dappled the floor. We were free, but we had only a room, not a home or security. We spent six years in limbo on Broizemer Strasse.

****

I couldn't wait to start school. I had a new dress and shoes, and my mother fussed my hair into long ringlets. Because my father taught me to read, write and do simple arithmetic, I began my formal schooling in the third grade. At school, we practiced reading, learned to spell, had our religious education classes, and learned the usual things kids in elementary school learn. A valiant, dedicated Polish woman attempted to teach us English from a book, but because her own command of the English language was so poor, we learned little. I learned English later by watching television and listening to my children. An English immersion course.

I finished grade six after only two years, and my formal education ended. A few students went to camps that taught the higher grades, but I was too young to leave my parents.

I am sitting in the last row, second from the left.

Warneck private collection

One time we three received the same dress in the same pattern. I am on the right, Lodzia in the middle and Josephine is on the left

Warneck Private Collection

UNRRA supplied us with clothing and household goods. Every month each refugee received a small stipend to spend as he or she wished. I liked to buy trinkets in the town shops. The Braunschweig Displaced Persons Camp was our home from 1945 until 1951.

My sister and I didn't concern ourselves with the future. Daddy and Mom worried enough for both of us. We had dances to attend, and ball games to play. We concentrated on being young and having fun. Parents didn't trust the Germans, so we always went into Braunschweig with a group of friends. We went to the movies, or the downtown park. Sometimes we went to the swimming pool and swam in our clothes. We didn't have bathing suits. About two weeks after we moved to the camp, my new friends and I walked to Braunschweig to explore. A convoy of troops drove by and tossed us candy. The American soldiers laughed and waved at us. Giggling like the school girls we were, we waved back at those good-looking boys. We were in high spirits, laughing and waving to the troops and scooping up the candy, especially the chocolate bars. As Poles, we were happy to be free, happy to receive greetings from the soldiers, and jubilant to get chocolate. One soldier riding on the back of a truck, tossing candy toward us, was an African-American. What I remember most vividly was his beautiful smile. His smile was broad showing the whitest teeth I had ever seen. He was the first person I ever saw with skin color different from mine.

****

We were encouraged to do the things most kids do while growing up. I studied my lessons, joined a singing group, and took part in many camp activities. A Polish music professor began our choir. He played the piano and sang in a mellow tenor voice. He brought the chorus together and taught us how to sing. One Christmas Eve, we sang at Midnight Mass. Before the final blessing, our Priest, Father Doboszcz, thanked us.

He spoke to the congregation, "Our choir has added glory and beauty to our blessed Christmas mass tonight." He turned and bowed toward us, "Thank you!" The worshipers stood and applauded us for several minutes.

We put on plays and performed for family and friends in the camp's all-purpose building. I loved entertaining, and appearing on stage. Applause from an audience set my heart singing. Popular music drifted through the camp and young people danced to folk tunes and modern music imported from the United States and Europe. Fiddlers played well-known dance songs. Lodzia learned to Jitterbug and became quite good at it. All the boys liked to dance with her.

****

Mrs. Brown, our teacher, loved poetry. She was talented, and she was well educated. I loved listening to her read and recite. She was our drama coach as well. Once she wrote a poem about me. It read in part that I was a "happy go-lucky little girl, with a bright smile," she said, "Vicky loves to dance!" Mrs. Brown asked me to perform in nearly every play we staged.

With Mrs. Brown. I am wearing a Polish national costume, and the boots my father had made for me. My mother is watching out the window.

Warneck private collection

On many occasions, we danced to compositions by Krakowiak, and Mazur as entertainment for the camp residents.

****

I joined the camp's Girl Scout troop. When I wore my uniform, I always felt important and part of something bigger. Our skirts were blue, the color of the sky, and we wore white jackets with blue stripes. Sky blue neckties completed the outfit. We wore the uniforms to Scout meetings, parades and for special occasions. Regina, our Scout leader wore the same uniform as we did, most of the time. UNRRA gave my father a greenish-brown shirt with shiny brass buttons. The shirt looked like something an important person would wear. Regina borrowed the shirt when she wanted to look more like our Scout leader than an overage Girl Scout. After Regina borrowed it a few times my father gave it to her.

This is my Girl Scout Troop. I am in the middle and Regina stands off on the left.

Warneck private collection

Regina made a lovely blue dress for me. She embroidered the skirt with bright, delicate flowers. Once, I wore it dancing a solo performance in front of the audience. Regina was an enthusiastic, creative Scout leader. We were regular Girl Scouts and worked on the same kinds of projects as Girl Scouts worldwide did then and now.

Some of many memorable times we had were the camping trips Regina arranged for us at Harz Mountain, Germany. Harz Mountain was a wonderful, magical place and we loved spending time there. We slept in two hotels built for tourists before the War. Two German grandmothers did most of the cooking. The older of the two, Hildegarde, sang in the kitchen as she worked. Hildegarde did not speak Polish, but most of us spoke enough broken German to say a few words to her. Hildegarde made delicious strudel with what she had available. She used berries or apples, or savory wild mushrooms grown on the mountain. She seemed to enjoy spending time with us. The other cook, Henrietta, didn't smile, and her gruff manner scared some of the girls. When the cooks were absent, we cooked over a campfire. We picked blueberries and wild raspberries and ate them long before we got back to camp.

Bonfires chased off the evening's chill. We sang Polish folk songs and the modern songs we heard at camp. And we danced! Sometimes the Boy Scouts and their leaders joined us. Generally, we stayed on Harz Mountain for a week, but sometimes we stayed longer. During the summer months, the days were long, and the mountain air was cool. For a time we forgot the ugliness of the War, and the bleakness of the camp. We delighted in the beauty of the natural world, and the time we spent together.

Before the invasion, Mom and I went into the forest behind our house and picked mushrooms. Mom taught me how to tell edible mushrooms from those that were poisonous. Those lessons came in handy when the Girl Scouts were at Harz Mountain. I picked wild mushrooms, and brought them back to the old hotel. I threaded the window to dry. Back at the barracks, Mom fried the dried mushrooms with onions, and we ate them with black bread and cheese. Ah, they were so good!

My Girl Tro
with some of t
Boys Scouts a
their leaders.
am third fro
the right, a
Regina
standing next
me.

Warneck private collection

After we finished our educations, my friends Maria, Evelina and I went to see Heizal the seamstress and Peter the tailor in their shop. We asked them if they would teach us to sew. (Maria and Evelina were both common Polish names. It was coincidental that their names were the same as each of my grandmothers.) Heizal was in her late thirties. Peter was in his fifties and recognized as an excellent tailor. Heizal and Peter were Polish speaking German nationals. They agreed to teach us. Our regular hours were from nine to four. We earned no wages, but we learned a useful trade.

The shop had two large rooms, one served as Heizal's apartment. Two windows allowed natural light to pour into our workshop. We worked at oversized tables cutting material and laying out patterns. Those tables, two sewing machines, and a few chairs filled the room. Heizal taught me to turn collars, hem garments and make buttonholes.

After I mastered those skills, she taught me to add finishing touches to dresses and suits. I made myself two dresses under her direction.

Heizal didn't share her personal life. When I came to work in the morning, I often saw her boyfriend, Krajewski, in his pajamas drinking a cup of coffee. Heizal took good care of her lover. She baked sweets that perfumed the air in the sewing room, but she offered nothing to us.

Heizal is standing behind the dog. Krajewski is next to her, Peter the tailor is next to Krajewski. Evelina is behind the sewing machine, and Maria is hand sewing. The person next to Evelina is unknown. I am not in this picture.

Warneck private collection

In 1947, Europe faced critical food shortages because of War's destruction, and by the harsh winter and spring weather of 1946 and

1947. Finding fresh fruits or vegetables in the market was cause for celebration.

Centuries before the War, Braunschweig governors gave residents a piece of land to farm on in the outskirts of the town. Ownership of the plots was passed down through generation to generation. Tall fencing surrounded our camp, but the enclosure did not block the view of flourishing orchards and abundant vegetable gardens. During the growing season, we watched urban farmers bicycle or walk to their thriving patches. They left with baskets full of carrots and cabbages, apples and pears but they gave nothing to the hungry faces on the other side of the fence.

A carefully tended garden and orchard grew on the eastern side of the camp's high fence. One August morning, with the sun promising a hot day, I spotted a group of my friends slipping through a hole in the fence.

It looked interesting. "Hey, what are you guys doing?"

"Victoria, there are ripe cherries on those trees! We are going to pick some."

"You are?" I wanted cherries too. I followed the boys through the jagged opening into the orchard. What I didn't know was the landowner was working in his tool shack.

The owner saw us and yelled, "Hey you! You kids! What are you doing? Get away from my cherry trees you little bastards. Get out of my garden."

The angry, red faced, grey haired farmer with an obvious limp chased us through the orchard back toward the fence. His limp didn't slow him down. *What if he catches me?* The boys ran faster than I did, and they squirmed back through the fence hole before the farmer caught them. I was inches away from escape when a strong hand grabbed my shoulder.

The boys shouted, "Vicky, run away! Vicky, run away!" But the farmer had a firm grip on me and I couldn't run away.

The farmer shouted at me, "What are you doing, you thief? I am turning you over to the guards. You and your friends are thieves! You'll to be sorry you stole from me."

"Let me go! You're hurting me!" I yelled, but he didn't loosen his grip. I sobbed the whole way. My legs felt rubbery. *What would to happen to me? Would I go to jail?*

In 1945, Allied Military Police guarded the camp's entrances. As American and British soldiers withdrew Poles with military or law enforcement experience took over sentry duties. Still, anyone wearing a uniform frightened me.

The landowner dragged me to the guardhouse.

The guard at the gate looked at me and listened while the farmer complained, "Kids from this camp are stealing cherries off of my trees, and vegetables from my garden. I caught this one red-handed. You are supposed to supervise these brats. Those are my trees, my berries and my vegetables, keep those thieves off my property!"

I hung my head and told the guard, "I didn't even have one cherry, I didn't take anything, and he chased me."

The sentry told the angry farmer, "Don't worry, I'll take care of this." The farmer shook his fist, and turned back toward his garden. The guard ushered me in through the front door of the guardhouse. I didn't know what he planned do. My knees were shaking. Inside the shack, the security guard laughed and opened the shack's back door and ushered me out. I thought nothing that happened to me that day was funny.

I asked my friends, "Why didn't you tell me there was a German there?"

They laughed at me. Those boys made me so angry I didn't talk to them for a week. The next day the German farmer mended the hole in his fence.

We continued to pilfer fruits and vegetables from our German neighbors. We slipped into orchards and picked fruit off laden trees or swiped potatoes, onions and carrots from vegetable plots. On one occasion, I filled my sack full of crimson, crunchy apples and took them home.

Mom asked me, "Where did you get all these apples?"

"We went to a German's orchard and picked them off the trees."

Mom shook her head. But, her concern wasn't that I'd stolen the apples.

She said in a stern tone, "Next time you ask me or your father if you can go off with those kids."

My mother knew a local farmer who gave her carrots and potatoes and an occasional onion. We couldn't store much in our one room. Even when meat and butter became plentiful, we had no refrigerator to keep food cold.

****

After years of wear, my father's once handsome hand sewn leather boots were beyond repair. He had mended them many times. He borrowed a thick sharp needle from the shoemaker and sewed split seams. Daddy reattached loose soles using strong glue that had the sweet aroma of almond paste. Leather was scarce, and it took weeks for the shoemaker to get enough material to make him a new pair. Made from supple leather, buffed to the color of mahogany, they were warm, sturdy, and well made. Daddy was so happy with his comfortable boots he decided I would have a pair just like his.

"Daddy, your new boots are very nice, but they aren't the kind the girls wear. My friends will see my boots and laugh at me, Daddy."

He insisted, "You'll be happy you have them, Victoria, in the winter when snow covers the ground."

As usual, he was right. The unfashionable boots kept my feet warm and dry all winter. I just made sure my friends didn't see me wearing them.

****

Mom found work as a laundress in the hospital laundry. Her hands were rough and chapped from the strong soap and bleach used to presoak bedding and towels before washing. When the linens were dry, Mom ironed the sheets, pillowcases and flat pieces into neat rectangles.

My favorite piece of equipment was the soaking tub.

When my mother was working, I'd go to the laundry and coax her, "Please, please Mom, put hot water in there and let me take a bath." I loved climbing into the tub of hot, soapy water and lounging about until the water got cold and my fingers looked like ten wrinkled prunes. That was heaven. Mom worried she'd lose her job if we were caught. But I told her, "Mama, what are they going to do if they catch us? You're working here, washing and ironing. I'm just taking a bath."

****

Fathers, husbands and sons who had worked hard all their lives had nothing to do. There was no steady work for them in the camp. Bored, many of them met in a nearby field, passing the time by playing cards.

I usually came home from school hungry, and looked for something to eat. I was a slender, lanky young girl getting taller by the day.

Daddy teased me about my appetite, "You are always hungry!" One afternoon after school, Daddy left his card game and came to check on me.

"I'm hungry, Daddy."

"I'm hungry too. We have a little bacon, and a loaf of black bread. You fry the bacon and make sandwiches for us. Call me when the sandwiches are ready."

Daddy went back to his card game.

I put a small skillet on the hot plate and added the slabs of bacon. My stomach growled fueled by my hunger and the aroma's coming from the pan. I wanted to hurry the cooking, so I pushed the bacon into the hot grease using a fork. In an instant fat splashed onto my arm. In pain and panicking I ran around the small room flailing my arm. That made the burning worse. I remembered to take the skillet off the heat and ran to the medical clinic.

The doctor asked, "What happened to you? How did you get this burn?"

"I was frying bacon for Daddy and me," I said, "and grease splashed on my arm."

"You have an ugly, deep tissue burn, it is blistering." The doctor gently spread an orange salve over my injury and covered the wound with sterile gauze.

"Don't get the dressing wet and come back to see me in a week," he ordered.

My mother came home from work and saw the sterile bandages on my arm.

"I was hungry after school, so I was cooking bacon for Daddy and me," I said.

Before I could finish my sad story, Mom shouted at my father, "You play cards all day long. You cannot even make your daughter a sandwich when she is hungry. She had to feed you! You lazy so and so! Here I am trying to do good for the family. Instead of you, I'm doing it!"

My burned arm started the biggest argument of their married life.

****

Father Doboszcz loved the Lord and each of us. Everyone who lived or worked at the camp became a member of his flock. None of my classmates had been confirmed, some hadn't made their first Holy Communion, and children born in Germany had yet to be baptized. Father taught us religious education and prepared us to receive the Sacraments. He was a strict but kind and patient teacher. Father was a small man proud of his Polish military service as a chaplain. Arrested for resisting the Nazi invasion, he spent years at Dachau as a political prisoner. Starvation, disease and vermin dogged the Polish priests over the twelve years Dachau was in operation. Throughout his years of imprisonment, Father Doboszcz never lost sight of his calling or abandoned his faith.

More than a hundred priests and at least two bishops celebrated the Mass in a huge soccer stadium in Braunschweig on the Sunday of my Confirmation. Thousands of people filled the huge stadium from all over Europe. The Braunschweig facility was just one of many DP camps. Father Doboszcz was one of many priests celebrating the mass on that warm, sunny, happy day. The day was perfect, and it has remained a bright, shiny, memory for me.

Father Doboszcz in the classroom dressed in his Army uniform.

Warneck private collection

Eventually, Farther Doboszcz immigrated to Cleveland, Ohio where he celebrated the fiftieth anniversary of his ordination into the priesthood.

Father Doboszcz is second from the left, sitting with teachers from our school. Warneck private collection

****

My sister was a teenager when we went to Braunschweig. Lodzia went to dances, and she dated many Polish boys. She was a pretty, slight girl with light brown hair and sparkling brown eyes. Lodzia had an army of friends. We each took after our mother and loved dancing and singing. As young people do, Lodzia and a young Polish boy fell in love, and they wanted to marry. Lodzia's young man went to my father to ask for her hand. My father listened, but he had little to say. The boy told him his plans for their future, "I'm going back to my family's farm in Poland soon, and I want Lodzia to go with me as my wife."

Daddy looked at the two of them for a few minutes. He wasn't smiling.

"I don't have any problem with your getting married, but Lodzia is not going back to Poland."

My sister started to cry; the boy began to argue, but my father was resolute.

"No daughter of mine is going back to Poland. There will be new troubles there. The Poland we knew is gone and the Sielicki family is not going back."

That was the end of the engagement.

The boy returned to Poland and after Lodzia recovered from her heartbreak, she dated other young men. Then she found Stanislaw.

A few days before my sister's wedding I still wore bandages over my burned arm. I was a bridesmaid. *How can I be in Lodzia's wedding wearing these bandages?* I worried, cried and complained, but the burn healed none the faster, and my arm remained wrapped in a sterile dressing on the day of the big event. Our friends and relatives came to see Lodzia and Stanislaw get married and to enjoy the wedding reception. Few guests paid attention to the bandages on my arm. It was Lodzia and Stanislaw's big day.

Father Doboszcz married Lodzia and Stanislaw in the camp's social hall. She was a young, beautiful bride, and her husband a handsome, gallant young man. They had a lively Polish wedding. Neighbors brought fiddles and accordions so we had music for dancing. The wedding guests brought the feast. We ate our fill of kielbasa and black bread and the men drank homemade vodka and rum. I was self-conscious because bandages still covered my burned arm but when the wedding and the festivities began, I forgot all about my bandages and had a lot of fun.

Stanislaw's friend Piotr made the first toast to the bride and groom. After the toast, we sang a traditional Polish song called

Sto lat, with the words "Good health, good cheer, may you live a hundred years, one hundred years."

My parents were happy for Lodzia and Stanislaw, their only reservation was that Lodzia was very young. She was eighteen years old.

A year later Lodzia and Stanislaw welcomed a baby boy they called Mietek. He was a bright, sunny baby, and we all him adored him. They lived in a barracks two buildings away from ours. I visited Lodzia, Stanislaw and Mietek often. I loved singing to my little nephew. Later, when he started to walk, we danced around the tiny room. Lodzia laughed watching us, and Mietek laughed too.

****

Two weeks after Lodzia married Stanislaw, his sister Josephine, wed an engineer. Her mother arranged a marriage for her to a man nearly twice her age. Sixteen-year-old Josephine had no choice but to marry him. Josephine asked Wanda, and Helina and me to be her bridesmaids. The male members of the wedding party were friends of the groom.

On Josephine's wedding day the good-looking men escorted the bridesmaids to the church. I felt so grown-up walking beside an attractive, older man. At the reception, everyone danced to accordion music. I swirled and twirled in a new dress. Uninvited boys our age watched through the windows and saw us smiling and dancing. We three girls worked even harder at having a good time trying to make those boys jealous. The bride was miserable, but her bridesmaids had a wonderful time.

After the wedding, Josephine and her new husband went to live at another camp. Occasionally, they came back to visit, and she saw her friends. She was unhappy and cried telling us about her marriage. Josephine and her husband had two sons and two daughters after they immigrated to Australia. One of her friends who kept in touch with her told me Josephine's husband abused her and she divorced him. Later, she had a child with her second husband. I hope she is still happy.

Here I am at twelve or thirteen. My long hair was worn in schoolgirl braids.
Warneck private collection

****

In 1947, I was thirteen and I kept getting sick. Every few weeks I would develop a severe sore throat and run a fever. My mother took care of me until the time I was so sick she was afraid for me and took me to the camp's medical clinic. I was quarantined and put to bed on cot in a small room. Not only was I sick, I was miserable. I missed my friends. I couldn't go to school or with the Girl Scouts camping or take part in a lot of fun things that my troop planned to do. I was out of commission for the entire week, the longest week of my childhood in the camp.

A classmate of mine, Irene, kept getting severe sore throats and fevers too. She and I missed quite a lot of school because we were too sick to attend. Irene's parents, Mr. and Mrs. Perdenia, both taught at the school. Mom and Daddy, and Irene's parents talked to each other and agreed that something had to be done. Irene's mother arranged for us to see a German throat specialist who practiced in the town of Braunschweig.

The doctor examined my throat and shook his head. He recommended surgery.

"Vicky's tonsils are infected and they keep making her sick. They are not doing their job. I think they should be removed so she doesn't keep getting sick from the infection." The doctor examined Irene and came to the same conclusion. We needed to have surgery.

Our parents took us to a small clinic where the same doctor did our surgeries. Irene and I had the operation on the same day. We were both afraid, and our mothers tried to calm our fears. The surgery went without a hitch, and both sets of parents heaved sighs of relief. After surgery, a nurse put us in a little room with two beds. The feather beds had clean, starched and ironed white sheets. Those beds were a luxury for both of us. My bed at camp was a simple cot with blankets provided by UNRRA. Our throats were sore, and the nurse gave us ice water to ease the discomfort of swallowing. We stayed for a week that seemed to me longer than seven days. The doctor came in to check on us once or twice a day, and a nurse was there around the clock.

My parents never received a bill from the doctor or the clinic. I don't know why. Anyway, I was too young and too sick to worry about how much the surgery cost. Maybe the German surgeon felt sorry for us, or maybe the Allies insisted that he treat us. When I came back to our room in the barracks, my mother fixed soft foods and soups for me until my throat healed. We didn't have any popsicles and ice cream was a rare delicacy. In a village about a kilometer from the camp, a man churned ice cream on special occasions. Kids of all makes and models lined up and hoped this heavenly delight wouldn't be gone before it reached them. That is the only time I remember having ice cream while we lived at the camp.

Months later a day came when my stomach hurt, and I was sick with diarrhea and vomiting. My mother was worried and took me to the camp clinic. A nurse put me to bed in the clinic for the night. The next morning, I started my first period. I was nearly fourteen years old.

****

My father's sister, Ksqwerka and her husband Alex had three children. A boy Mietek, a daughter Ewa and a little boy they named Wicus. Life takes unusual twists and turns, and Ksqwerka, Alex and their children ended up in our camp. Wicus was a thin, small child. His complexion had a grey cast to it, and he often complained to his parents of a stomachache. Wicus was smart, and he loved spending time with my father. Like my father, Wicus loved politics.

He asked, "Why do you want to go to America? How will you get there? Are the people nice? Is America different from Germany?"

My father loved the little boy, the son he never had. Wicus came to our room almost every day, or my father went to see him. Then Wicus got sick.

His parents took him to a doctor in Braunschweig for testing and treatment. The diagnosis was not good; Wicus had cancer of the stomach. I went to the hospital with my Aunt Ksqwerka to visit him. It was sad to see him lying in that little bed.

I said, "Aunt Ksqwerka, why don't you bring him home? Don't leave him here."

The next day his parents brought Wicus home to the camp and made him as comfortable as they could.

I don't know how or when he saw my little Christmas ornaments, but he asked about them.

"I like those Christmas decorations you have. They are so beautiful."

I got the little box of decorations and took it to him. Looking at them made him smile. I left the box of decorations with his mother.

A few days later Wicus passed away.

Everyone grieved at his loss. Father Doboszcz, the camp's priest celebrated the Mass of the Angels. The chapel filled to overflowing with people and children from the camp. We buried Wicus in the cemetery in Braunschweig. We had to leave him there. It makes me sad knowing he has no family buried near him.

The camp's chapel
It was filled to overflowing for Wicus's funeral.

Warneck private collection

Survivors living in the DP camp often shared their tragic, traumatic War stories with us. Chester Basinski's mother shared one such tragic episode. Chester and I were friends, but not girlfriend and boyfriend. We were youngsters happy that the War was over, and we were still alive. Chester's mother cried as she told us what happened to her husband.

"Ukraine murderers rode their horses onto our farm at dawn. My husband was working near the barn, and saw them riding hard toward him." He yelled to me, "Run! Take Chester and hide. Hurry. Go! Run!"

"I grabbed Chester and we ran, I thought my husband was behind us." She stopped to wipe her tears. "I looked back toward the house and saw a raider knock him to the ground. Three of the Ukrainians jumped off their horses, hammered him with rifle butts, and kicked him with heavy boots. Even after he did not move anymore, they kept beating him. I held Chester to my breast so he couldn't see what was happening to his father. I did not want my son's last memory of his Daddy to be of him being beaten to death. The bastards looted the house and the barn, taking what they wanted, and destroying the rest. When it got dark, Chester and I slipped out of our hiding place in the forest and went back to the house. Chester cried himself to sleep in my arms. I put him to bed, and took the blanket off our bed. I used it to cover my husband's bloody, broken body. In the barn, our cow and goat lay dead. The butchered carcasses left to rot. The next morning men from the village came and helped me bury my husband. Now when I close my eyes I see the murderers killing him. We will never go back to Poland."

****

When my Uncle Edwin, and my Grandmother Evelina, announced they were returning to Poland, it broke my father's heart. Uncle Edwin had married and fathered a young son they called Jan. My mother and father and his sister, Ksawerka, pleaded with them to come to America, but to no avail.

"Poland went to the Communists. You hate them as much as I do. Now you want to go and live with them?" My father asked.

My uncle would not listen. He took his family and my grandmother Evelina back to Poland. They left Braunsweig the next day. My father cried. I had never seen him with tears on his face before that day.

We were able to stay in touch with Uncle Edwin and his family after they left Germany for Poland. Their family grew, and they had four sons and one daughter. Uncle Edwin wrote the sad news that Grandmother Evelina died soon after they returned to Poland.

Life in Poland was gray and grim under the regime of the Ukraine Soviet Socialist Government. My parents had nothing extra, but they shared what they had. They sent packages of food and clothing to them. Daddy never forgave his brother for not coming to America. In 1954, my mother went to Poland to visit Edwin and his family, and she saw the hardships and challenges they faced every day.

****

The United States Congress passed the Displaced Person's Act of 1948, granting entry into the United States for 227,000 displaced persons. The Germans called these people *ostarbeiter*, or eastern workers, most were Polish citizens who were forced to Germany to work for the Third Reich.

People with relatives living in the States were first in line to be resettled. Immigration to the United States was limited to refugees living in resettlement camps in 1945. Refugees were required to have a sponsor who guaranteed them a place to live and a job. A farmer living in Virginia sponsored Stanislaw, Lodzia and Mietek. So the day came in 1950 when we said a tearful good-bye to them and they boarded a train to begin the journey to the United States. In America Stanislaw's name became Stanley, Mietek was Michael and Lodzia was Lucy. Every week we said good-bye to people going to a new country or returning to their homeland. The USA, Canada, England, Brazil and Australia accepted Eastern European refugees. And some refugees made the decision to return to Poland.

****

Mrs. Basinski, the young mother who watched Ukraine criminals murder her husband, took Chester and resettled in New Zealand. Before they departed, my friend came to say goodbye and he gave me a beige chiffon kerchief decorated with tiny designs in green, black and red to wear over my hair.

"Vickie, I want you to have this. Every time you wear it you will think of me."

The material is thin now, but I have cherished that little gift through the years. I carefully fold it in tissue paper and put it away in my dresser drawer with other mementos. Chester was right. When I look at the scarf, I always think of him. I hope he has a good life in New Zealand, or wherever they are.

****

The hardest part of living at the camp was watching our family and friends leave. We didn't know if we would ever see any of them again, and not knowing if we would ever leave Germany. We wished them good fortune and waved enthusiastic goodbyes as their trains pulled away from the depot. I moped around for days after each parting.

Lodzia, Mom and Daddy, and me. The picture was taken while we lived in the DP camp in Germany.
Warneck private collection

In the middle of March 1951, it was our turn to leave. We waved goodbye to relatives and friends, and boarded the same train we had watched depart so many times before. We were on our way to Bremerhaven. The train was old and dirty. It belched black coal smoke from its stack as it rattled and creaked its way west. Wooden slat seats lined both sides of the train with an aisle in the center. By the end of the five-hour trip, my skinny bottom hurt.

From the depot in Bremerhaven, we bounced along sitting on an ancient bus that took us to a medical facility a few miles north of the city. The following week, after receiving complete physical examinations, the American doctors pronounced us healthy enough for an ocean voyage and for life in the United States. We received the grand prize of a boarding pass for the U.S.N.S. General C.H. Muir and a visa giving us entry into the United States.

The General Muir didn't come with creature comforts. It was a no-frills troop ship, designed to carry thousands of men to war. During the War, she carried troops to Pearl Harbor, the islands of Ulithi, Leyte, to the Philippines and other Pacific ports. She took thousands of refugees to America under the umbrella of the International Refugee Organization, and thousands more to Australia and the other nations who opened their borders to displaced European people. A few years later, the ship transported combat troops to Korea. She was awarded two battle stars for her service.

On March 31, 1951 Mom, Daddy and I were three of between 800 and 1,000 immigrants boarding the General C.H. Muir. I was sixteen. Many different languages speaking at the same time made the gangway sound like the Tower of Babel. Excitement was widespread, but an undercurrent of apprehension and anxiety simmered below the surface.

On the first day at sea, we sailed from Bremerhaven to the English Channel. Sailors and refugees stood on deck as we passed through the channel and out into the Atlantic. Men, women and children stood in tearful silence on the deck watching land fade from sight. The mass of refugees were somber, subdued by the unspoken realization that many would never return.

The ship's food was plain and abundant. We hadn't eaten that well since our evacuation to Germany. The vegetables and fruits we'd pilfered from the farmers around the Braunschweig camp were beneficial, but we could not steal enough to satisfy our starved appetites. I tasted my first orange and my first banana sailing on the General Muir. We bought Cokes from a machine for five cents each.

What luxury! Katrina, a Romanian girl with deep brown eyes and long dark hair and I met standing at a table in the mess hall on our first day on board. We were both teenagers and about the same age. Although I didn't speak Romanian and Katrina didn't speak Polish, we communicated using the German we knew, and a lot of body language. Katrina and I went on great adventures investigating the ship.

The General C.H. Muir. The ship that brought us to America in 1951. Wikipedia

It was not an easy crossing. The first three days the weather was beautiful with sunny skies and calm seas. Then conditions changed. We sailed through days of rough seas and high winds and cold, stinging rain. Most of us had never been on an ocean going ship. So many passengers were seasick it was hard to find a place at the rail, and sailors weren't able to keep the decks clean. The aroma of coffee and food floated from the galley, and there was plenty of food available, but the passengers were too sick to eat. I stayed away from the big deck vents and the stomach-turning odors and gasoline fumes that poured out of them. We spent several days in misery before the ocean calmed down and the land-lovers began to feel better.

We slept in two large but poorly lit compartments, males in one and females in the other. The cots were stacked four high and filled the space. We squeezed between the bunks banging shins and stubbing toes only to climb onto an uncomfortable cot. Body odors assailed every nose. Mom, Daddy and I slept out on deck when it wasn't raining or spitting snow. Cold seeped through our blankets in the early spring on the North Sea, but it was better than trying to sleep below decks.

The Captain hosted a party in the largest dining room for us the night before we docked in New York City. We ate a variety of sandwiches and drank soft drinks and coffee. There was even cake. The best part was the music, all kinds of music, for dancing. Sailors brought accordions, Polish refugees played tambourines and Polish fiddles. Katrina and I laughed, danced and ate until the wee hours of the morning.

The next day we sailed past the Statue of Liberty and into the harbor. Hundreds of people were outside on deck as we glided by Lady Liberty. Smiles and tears of happiness highlighted weary faces, and we offered prayers thanking God for safe passage and for this opportunity to live in freedom in this great nation.

We disembarked the General Muir and entered the U.S. customs building in New York City. Once again, doctors examined us to confirm we were healthy enough to enter the country.

After passing through customs and immigration, I asked Daddy, "Will you give me a nickel for a Coke?"

A man from the Polish Immigration Association approached my father and spoke with him at length. He gave Daddy sixty-five dollars. The man, I never learned his name, took us to Grand Central Station and put us on a train to Roanoke, Virginia, where Lucy, Stanley and Michael met us at the depot. It was April 10, 1951. My father was not one to accept charity and at the first opportunity, he repaid the Polish American Society the money they gave us.

We lived with Lucy and Stanley in a tiny Roanoke apartment for six months. There was so little room Mom and Daddy slept in the garage.

Mom stayed home and took care of my sister's little boy, Michael. Lucy, Stanley, Daddy and I found jobs and went to work.

Daddy found a job as a hired hand on a large Virginia farm. He loved farming, but the snakebite that nearly killed him was never far from his mind. Every day, snakes with different markings crossed his path. Daddy both hated and feared them. Virginia snakes were unfamiliar to him. He did not know which were poisonous and which were harmless, and his English was not good enough to ask questions.

None of us was happy with our situation. We learned of friends who were living in a Polish community in New Jersey. I wrote a letter to one of the friends I made in Braunschweig. I said we were saving money so we could move to New Jersey, too. Our Polish friends sent a truck to Roanoke to get us. I rode to Dunellen, New Jersey in the bed of a pick-up truck. Mom and Lucy took turns holding Michael in the truck's cab.

****

In New Jersey, we settled into our new lives. My father found a job in a foundry, and Mom worked in a little factory that sewed dresses. I was hired by Kingston Connelly to wrap cores for electrical appliances. Two years after I was hired, Howell Electric bought Kingston Connelly. I worked for Kingston Connelly for two years and Howell Electric for sixteen years.

The law stated we had to be in the United States for five years before we could become American citizens. In 1956, our entire family went to the New Brunswick, New Jersey courthouse and became naturalized American citizens. That was one of the happiest days in our lives.

****

My father's goal in America was to own his own house. I gave him my paycheck every week, and within a year's time Daddy had saved enough to put down a deposit on a small house. I was working, Mom had a job, and Daddy was working. Less than two years later the house was owned free and clear.

****

Parties and dances were held somewhere in Dunellen every week. There were a lot of weddings and wedding receptions to attend as young men and women began to marry. Three wonderful children were born to me after I married.

My parents lived a good life, an American life. But, it did not last. Seven years after they bought their house, my father died of cancer. Mom died in 1989 of a heart problem, and Lodzia died of cancer in 1987. Lodzia's only child, Michael, died in an accident in 1984. I still grieve at their loss and I miss all of them every day of my life.

A NEW DAWN

The Polish government never surrendered to Germany, and Germany never formally declared war on Poland. The Polish Government in Exile operated in Great Britain until 1945. Sixteen squadrons of Polish pilots who were able to escape from occupied Europe flew with RAF pilots during the Battle for Britain. Due to the political climate of the times, these brave men were never publically acknowledged.

From the start of the occupation, men and women fought to regain Poland. Polish Resistance units are believed to have been the largest organized resistance movement in occupied Europe. Units sabotaged German supply lines, printed Polish newspapers and pamphlets, provided valuable military intelligence to the Allies and saved untold numbers of Jewish lives. Prewar Poland was destroyed and a new free nation has risen out of the ashes and thrives today. Poland's spirit lives on.

****

The Lysy family was our neighbors in Derazno. We knew they were sent to Germany, but we didn't know if any of them survived. Imagine our surprise when we found the whole family living in our camp. We were so happy to see each other! There were three sisters, Maria was the oldest, Sosia, and Helena. We went to school together. Their family left the camp two weeks earlier than we did. They didn't know where they would be settled in the United States, but they were eager and excited to be on their way. As luck would have it, the family resided in the same Polish community in Dunellen as we did. Maria and I renewed our friendship and attended each other's weddings. We remain friends and stay in touch with Christmas cards and occasional phone calls.

****

Uncle Mihal's oldest daughter, Amelia, married prior to the invasion. She and her husband went to Germany with Mihal and the rest of the family.

Somehow, Uncle managed to keep his family together. That was a miracle. Then one spring day in 1948, Mihal's and his entire family arrived at the Broizemer Strasse camp. We celebrated being together again, and caught up on how our families had survived. We had a lot to be grateful for. We had all survived. Mihal and Rosali had worked out their marital differences and had a beautiful, healthy baby girl. We celebrated Mihal's son Jon's marriage to Danusia during the war and the baby boy born of that union. The baby's name was Marin. When I was asked to be Marin's Godmother, I happily accepted. I felt very grown-up to be permitted to take on such an important responsibility. I was a very young Godmother.

Mihal and his extended family relocated to Chicago. Years later I went to Marin's wedding. It was a wonderful occasion where relatives and friends shared memories of the past and made plans for the future.

****

The summer of 1957, my family visited my father's sister and her husband in Norwich, Connecticut. I was admiring his huge garden when I noticed a tall mound in the back.

"Uncle, what do you have there?" He took me by the hand.

"Come, I'll show you," he said.

We walked almost to the end of his property, and I saw the well-planned, well-drained root cellar he had built. It was just like the root cellar we had in Poland. Three jars of canned tomatoes waited there ready for stuffed cabbage, or *Zupa pomidorowa*, tomato soup. Uncle stored potatoes, carrots, beets and onions there over the winter. Hay and straw protected his vegetables from bitter cold. My uncle told how in the spring, he and his family harvested fresh vegetables from the garden. In the summer, tomatoes, corn and green beans were canned and stored in the root cellar with the harvested vegetables.

My father and I sharing a happy moment in Dunellen, New Jersey.

Warneck private collection.

*****

In 2002 my cousin, Klara, and I visited Germany. As I grew older, memories often took on an odd dream like quality. It was important to me to know for certain what I remembered was the truth.

I was eager to see Modessa and the Gruber farm where I spent so much of my childhood. Only weeds and scruff grew in the once thriving fields, and no green beet tops pushed up through the soil. Scrub brush and wild saplings choked the orchards. The dilapidated house needed paint and some of its windows were broken. The back door we always used was off its hinges. Nature had taken charge of the once prosperous farm. Herr and Frau Gruber died in 1985 and 1986.

A tractor accident left Manfrit Gruber crippled. Manfrit's sister, Hannah, married a baker and moved to Hanover. Erica, who was the youngest Gruber child, moved to Berlin after she was grown. Her brother and sister lost contact with her. They didn't know where she was or what happened to her.

****

We stopped at the post office on Haupt Strasse for postcard stamps. The tall, blond counter clerk with startling blue eyes asked in a hushed voice, "Victoria? Victoria Sielicki? Is that you? Do you remember me? My mother was the postmistress during the War."

I had a hazy recollection of her son, Karl. He had just turned six when we left for Braunschweig. He could have been Hitler's Aryan poster boy with his white blond hair and blue eyes. When he was little his hair curled into little ringlets, and his mother told everyone she cried when her husband gave Karl his first haircut. I was surprised he remembered me at all; he was so young. Karl remembered my family worked for Herr Gruber. Karl and his wife treated us like old friends who stopped by on short notice. He invited us into his home and opened a bottle of Champagne. His wife served us bread and cheese. We spent well over an hour talking about our families and the people we knew. We talked about how hard life was during the War, and wha happened to us during the years after the War. I told him my family spent six years at the DP camp on Broizemer Strasse in Braunschweig. Karl remembered my parents and Lodzia. He told me his mother died in 1955. His father never returned from the War's Russian front.

We drove to the DP camp in Braunschweig and went to the building where my family lived. No more small rooms for housing families, the remodeled building now held offices. The chapel where we'd had mass contained rows of desks. The hall where we went to dances, and put on our plays was conference space. The streets seemed the same, but trees and shrubbery had matured. Colorful landscaping now softened the camp's sharp features.

Here I am standing beside the window of the small living space we had on Gruber's farm.

Warneck private

****

So that was my youth. I made many good friends along the way. Girl Scouts and schooling allowed me to have the childhood I'd been denied even though it came later than most.

Sometimes I felt my life was spent saying goodbye. Watching my friends and relatives leave for other places was the saddest, hardest part. My friends went all over the world. Some returned to what was left of Poland. I stay in touch with a few who came to America. We write letters to each other, and visit over the phone.

I am a survivor. Even during the War, I knew how to take care of myself. I trusted my own instincts. I knew I would never get lost or go hungry again. I'd manage something.

In our family, we always had God in our lives. We prayed before sleep each night and gave thanks for our many blessings. We thanked God for survival every day we were in Germany. Mom taught me to pray and grounded me in the deep faith I practice every day. I think the reason I've lived so many years is to share our family's story, for we must never forget.

Victoria Sielicki Warneck
March 2016

ABOUT THE AUTHORS

Victoria Sielicki Warneck lives in South Carolina with her husband, Alan. She is active in her church, and she loves to cook and share delicious Polish dishes and pastries. Victoria has made the United States her home since 1951. She became an American citizen in 1955.

Carole Reno Brier lives in South Carolina with her husband, Carey. She writes fiction, creative nonfiction, and biographies. She graduated from Trinity College in Burlington, Vermont.

Made in the USA
Charleston, SC
30 March 2016